THE RELIGIOUS LIFE OF
ANCIENT ROME

THE RELIGIOUS LIFE
OF ANCIENT ROME

A STUDY IN THE DEVELOPMENT OF
RELIGIOUS CONSCIOUSNESS
FROM THE FOUNDATION OF THE CITY
UNTIL THE DEATH OF GREGORY
THE GREAT

BY

JESSE BENEDICT CARTER

AUTHOR OF "THE RELIGION OF NUMA"

NEW YORK
COOPER SQUARE PUBLISHERS, INC.
1972

Originally Published, 1911
Reprinted 1972 by Cooper Square Publishers, Inc.
59 Fourth Avenue, New York, N. Y. 10003
International Standard Book Number 0-8154-0429-8
Library of Congress Catalog Number 72-84817

Printed in the United States of America

TO THE MEMORY OF
HERBERT FLETCHER DECOU

PREFACE

THE eight chapters of this book were originally eight lectures delivered before the Lowell Institute in Boston during January, 1911. Though they have been slightly recast, their character as lectures has been preserved, even at the risk of retaining statements which are more dogmatic than one would make in a book of essays written to be read. But the theory of religious evolution here developed is put forth in the hope that it may arouse thought and discussion; and to this end a positive statement seems desirable.

In the first three chapters I have made some use of my earlier book *The Religion of Numa;* and I wish to thank the Messrs. Macmillan for their kind permission to treat the same subject again in this connection. In the story of Christianity I have received much help from Monseigneur Duchesne's *Origines,* a book where profound and critical scholarship is marvelously blended with reverence and devotion. In the later period one is always unconsciously influenced by Gibbon, while Gregorovius and Hodgkin afford many valuable suggestions. I regret that Warde Fowler's *Religious Experiences of the Roman People* did not appear in time for me to make use of it.

I wish to thank President Lowell and Professor Sedgwick, Curator of the Institute, for their unfailing kindness during the delivery of the lectures, and Mr. James Ford Rhodes and Mr. Thomas Spencer Jerome for encouragement and suggestion in connection with the book.

. . . .

In the midst of the final draft came the news of the death at Cyrene of that profound scholar and lovable gentleman, Herbert Fletcher Decou. The book is dedicated to him as a token of my gratitude for the privilege of having been his friend.

JESSE BENEDICT CARTER.

HOSPENTHAL,
September, 1911.

CONTENTS

THE RELIGIOUS LIFE OF
ANCIENT ROME

THE RELIGIOUS LIFE OF
ANCIENT ROME

CHAPTER I

ROME AND THE ETRUSCANS: THE RELIGION OF AGRI-
CULTURE AND THE RELIGION OF PATRIOTISM

IT was in no spirit of idle boasting that Rome was called
the "Eternal City." This quality of eternity is manifest, not so much perhaps by Rome's great age as by her
ever-present youthfulness. But before all, it is in the
essential quality of continuity that her eternity receives
its largest measure of evident probability. For at least
three thousand years — barring one interruption of
forty days — human life in all its manifold phases has
been unfolding itself on these hills beside the Tiber, and
during nearly two thousand of these three thousand
years all the rest of our Western world has looked with
awe and reverence towards that place, and by reason of
its very longing to be present there, has felt in its heart
that vague anxiety that

> " I perchance shall never come
> To look on that so holy spot
> The very Rome."

Thus it is that thoughtful men have sought to find in
the history of Rome a kind of guidebook of human

experience. They found there the history of their own past, — for in an Occidental world we are all of us the spiritual children of Rome, entirely aside from our specific religious views or our specific physiological ancestry, — and they found it not in broken segments, but in the complete whole. It was but natural, therefore, that, so long as our concept of history consisted in the annals of wars and battles, Rome should be the great text-book of military history. And when we passed from this naïve conception to the study of men's political relations, it was equally natural that Rome should again be sought in the hope of finding there the story of man's political development. Yes, there were even especial reasons in this case because of the well-known talents of the Romans in the field of law and political organization.

But the study of the past has in recent years progressed beyond these formal relations, and we have come into the sociological age, when we wish to read our history, not in legal enactments, but in the pulse and tone of the masses, and even of the individuals who stood behind and beneath those laws and edicts. Finally, in this new century the more progressive minds have grown weary of playing with purely material things, rich and profitable as the harvest of those things has been, or even with matters which belong on the surface of psychology. As a result we find ourselves to-day in the presence of a widespread interest in those things which pertain to religion, to religion in its broadest sense, as a feeling of dependence upon the action of powers which are none the less real because they are in the main unknown, and incapable of tangible proof.

This present - day revival of religion has assumed a great variety of forms, giving rise in turn to those inevitable animosities, which have their source in the essentially individual and personal character of religious feeling. It is possible, however, at least for those who possess an intellectual balance, to rise temporarily above this strictly personal attitude, and to recognize the great truth that religion is a normal and essential part of our human existence, and that this has been true in all time, and that in all except the excessively material periods of human history, this religious instinct has been the greatest propulsive factor in our human psychology. Now, if this be true, we must to a certain extent rewrite our whole human history, not in the light of any specific religion, but in the recognition of the strength and validity of the religious instinct. In the past we have been given to the study of a particular religion or to that jejune discipline known as Comparative Religion. What we are to do now is to study not so much a religion in itself, but rather the effect of the impact of a specific religion upon the psychological consciousness of a people. Our interest is, therefore, not primarily in the content of the religion, but in the reaction which this content has called forth in any given set of human beings.

The history of Rome offers, perhaps, the best field in which to test the validity of these considerations. This book is the result of the experiment, but perhaps I should rather say that it is not so much the result of this experiment as the experiment itself which we are about to carry out.

But first it will be well to say a few words about the particular reasons why Rome offers such a peculiarly favorable field for our experiments. At first sight this would not seem to be the case. We are not accustomed to think of the Romans as a strongly religious people. Nor have the students of Roman religion, with a few exceptions, done anything to remove this prejudice. The religion of ancient Rome is very little known outside the narrow circle of specialists in Latin. Few attempts have been made to interpret it to the larger public. Even the students of the general history of religion know little of Rome, and do not ordinarily include her in their generalizations. Her religion has been hedged about in a very extraordinary way, as though the jealous secrecy, which was always a part of it in the days of its life, was still guarded after its death by the wraiths of the gods who have gone the way of all the earth. And yet Rome affords an extraordinary, even unique, opportunity for the prosecution of our task.

All religion is by nature conservative. In all its earlier stages, at least, it makes for solidarity, and this solidarity extends not only horizontally over the plane of the present, but it extends back into the third dimension of the past; and conservatism is a primary necessity for keeping in touch with the past. But in the case of Rome this conservatism, this faithfulness to the past, was felt to be of such great importance that it developed from the status of an accidental attribute into that of an essential quality and became by degrees almost the sum total of religion. The *mos majorum*, the custom of the fathers, was synonymous with religion, and piety had its psychological as well as its etymological truth in the relation of the younger generation to the older. But this conservatism is very precious to us in our study, for by it the successive strata of Rome's religious life were preserved, so that it may be said of her that in a sense she never lost any religious form, but kept them all intact until her latest days. This is quite a different matter from the inheritance of instinct which governs human life.

But it is not her conservatism alone which makes Rome so valuable for our purpose. There is the added fact of the richness and the variety of her religious experience. In these eight chapters we are to study that experience over a broad span of years, from the earliest times to the death of Gregory the Great, and we shall observe it unfolding itself before us. But it will

not detract from the dramatic power of that which we
are to study to come up for a moment into a high place
and look down upon the winding path which we are to
tread in the course of our investigation.

We see at first a primitive people, whose religion was
the reflex of their physical interests; we shall see them
dominated by a power farther advanced in civilization,
the Etruscans. We shall witness the birth of a new idea
of religion, the glorification of the State, the patriotic
instinct. We shall see the coming of another set of
influences, the presence of Greece, which was to soften
and civilize, but at the same time to engender a spirit
of skepticism. This spirit of skepticism was to be further strengthened by a marvelous growth of material
prosperity. Thus we reach the close of the Republic and
the religious conditions which are best reflected for us
in the person of Cicero.

Then the great change occurs, not primarily the
change from paganism into Christianity, but the change
from religion as first of all a social instinct into religion
as first of all an individual matter. We shall see at the
same time the rise of the idea of salvation, and we shall
witness the two contrary solutions of the problem, the
old Greek solution of salvation by knowledge and the
Oriental solution of salvation by faith. We shall then
behold the triumph of faith over knowledge in the
establishment of Christianity, and the reactionary triumph of mysticism over reason in the person of Julian.

Finally, the old patriotic instinct, which the Etruscans
first aroused, will reassert itself at the capture of Rome
by the Visigoths and we shall hear the answer of Augustine. But in spite of that answer, the social and
patriotic instincts of religion will triumph, and we shall
see at the end the wondrous way in which they received
their satisfaction in the presence of the unwitting Benedict and the prophetic Gregory.

The world's history offers no other such variety of
religious experience. Without this experience the conservatism of Rome would be of little use to us, for it
would preserve at best only a few forms of religious life.
While without the conservatism, the richness of the
experience would be lost for us, and only the latest forms
preserved. Our field, therefore, seems to have been
justly chosen, and we may go forward into the process
of our experiment.

The Roman people belong to what is known as the
Italic stock, a term by which we designate that particular offshoot of the great Aryan race, which came
down from the north into the peninsula of Italy. They
were not the first inhabitants, and they did not find the
peninsula empty. For lack of a better name, we call
the people who were there before them the "Western
Mediterranean" race. This original Mediterranean
people have left as a memorial of their one-time existence the dolmens and the nauraghi — the so-called
tombs of the giants — on Sardinia, Corsica, Malta, and

also on the mainland. It is possible that these people left the Mediterranean by following the coast line, and finally reached Gaul and Britain, where they are perhaps to be identified with the Druids, and if so, have left Carnac and Stonehenge as marks of their residence. But we know nothing of the religion of these people, nor is it likely that they would settle so far inland as the city of Rome. It is proper for us, therefore, to begin our story with the Italic stock.

These Italic people were doubtless scattered all through the highlands and lowlands of central and southern Italy, and like the beasts of the forest, seeking a salt lick, there would be a primitive traffic to the salt marshes, particularly at the mouth of the Tiber. Thus would come into existence the "Salt Road," the Via Salaria, probably the oldest of all the Roman roads. It is a curious fact that this Salt Road has always played an important part in Roman history, and the point where it enters Rome on the east has always been the vulnerable spot in her body. It was there that the Gauls came in B.C. 390, the Visigoths in A.D. 410, and the Italian troops in 1870.

We must not think of these people as a civilized folk, dwelling in cities, but rather as a barbarous or semi-barbarous aggregation inhabiting the hilltops, and surrounding their little groups of round huts by some sort of primitive palisade. None of the existing stone walls go back to this epoch, and this is not because these older walls have been destroyed, but because these people never built such walls. We have, however, memorials of their residence, that strange graveyard which was discovered some ten years ago in the Forum, near the foundations of the temple of Antoninus and Faustina. The earliest graves there go back into the ninth and possibly earlier centuries, and the latest burials seem to have taken place before the middle of the sixth century, when, as we shall see below, the region, in which this graveyard is found, became inclosed in the city wall. We know little of these people except their religion, but concerning that we are fairly well informed, thanks to their own conservatism and to our modern studies of primitive people.

The essential feature of their religion was its social character. Religion was not a personal matter, nay, it could not be, because the very concept of personality was in its infancy. There was no individual initiative or volition in the whole matter. Man did not choose his gods any more than he chose his parents. He was born into a circle of gods ready-made for him just as he was born into a set of human relationships. The fulfillment of his duty to those gods was a normal and natural function of his life. These gods were all about him. They were, to be sure, not gods in any developed sense; they were powers unknown except in so far as they manifested themselves in actions and things. The thing and the power that dwelt in it were inseparably connected. Yet the power was not the thing, nor was the thing the power. Janus was the door and yet not the door; Vesta the hearth and yet not the hearth. Janus was the power that manifested itself in the door. Thus with Janus were associated all the things that had to do with the door both in its physical and in its metaphysical aspects. Janus was the god of all entrances and of all beginnings, and thus also of the dawn as the beginning of the day, and of the New Year as the beginning of the year. Similarly, Vesta, who manifested herself in the hearth, became the goddess of all the family life which centred about the hearth.

Man felt himself surrounded by an infinite multitude of these powers. He strove to propitiate them and to establish an acceptable form of relationship between himself and them. Such a state of religion is usually called animism. It develops slowly into polytheism, when the spirit (*anima*) becomes named and then gradually better known; that is, when it becomes a god, in the more developed sense of the word. This process was actually fulfilled in the case of these settlers on the hilltops of Rome. Gradually this infinitude of unknown powers was transformed into a set of gods whose names were known. But these gods showed the limitations of their birth. Those who worshiped them knew them only in their activities. There was no play of speculation as to their character or their appearance. They were not thought of in the form of man, and no mythology or genealogy grew up about them. They were little more than names for powers, powers which must be put in motion for the benefit of the state.

In the intensity of the struggle for physical existence, these powers must be propitiated, that man and beast and Mother Earth might bring forth plentifully after their kind. This physical note, this instinct of propagation, is dominant in all the early religion of Rome. Let us examine it for a moment in its various phases. Before ever there was an organized state, before ever there was a settled monogamous family life, men were grouped together in brotherhoods, "curiæ." This organization continued to exist in later times, but it gradually lost its significance. In the curial worship we have the cult of Janus and Juno. This is the prototype of that cult of the Genius and the Juno which was carried on by each individual, the Genius of each individual man, the Juno of each individual woman. Reduced to its simplest terms, this is the worship of the Genius as the power of procreation, and of the Juno as the power of conception. But Janus is the great creator, the divine "Genius," and in his union with Juno in the curiæ we see the expression of the powers of physical reproduction.

Similarly in the other relations which sprang up subsequently, that of the gens, the family, and the state, we see the same physical interests. Even the memory of the dead is guided by the same principle. As there is no individual life on earth, neither is there any individual immortality after death. Each man at death passes over into the majority, that mass of good gods (*Di Manes*) who live the bloodless flitting life of the shades. But even here the universal principle of procreation is emphasized again, for these shades clamor for their rightful due, the sacrifice at the grave, and this sacrifice they accept only at the hands of their descendants. Thus across the life of every man who lives, lies the shadow of these shades, commanding him to reproduce after his kind, and thus to escape their wrath. It is little wonder, therefore, that all the other gods of this religion are marked with the same predominant purpose. They are gods of the flocks and of the crops. There is Faunus, who makes the cattle to breed; and Pales, who gives increase to the flock. There is Saturn, who looks after the sowing of the seed, Robigo, who keeps away the mildew; Consus, who guards the harvesting, and a host of others.

Yet for all this vital interest, this clinging as it were to the feet of the gods, we must not mistake its character. These people could know nothing of their gods, beyond the activity which the gods manifested in their behalf; nor did they desire to know anything. The essence of religion was the establishment of a definite legal status between these powers and man, and the scrupulous observance of those things involved in the contractual relation, into which man entered with the gods. As in any legal matter, it was essential that this contract should be drawn up with a careful guarding of definition, and an especial regard to the proper address. Hence the great importance of the name of the god, and failing that, the address to the "Unknown God." A prayer was therefore a vow (*votum*), in which man, the party of the first part, agreed to perform certain acts to the god, the party of the second part, in return for certain specified services to be rendered. Were these services rendered, man, the party of the first part, was *compos voti*, bound to perform what he had promised. Were these services not rendered, the contract was void. In the great majority of cases the gods did not receive their payment until their work had been accomplished, for their worshipers were guided in this by the natural shrewdness of primitive man, and experience showed that in many cases the gods did not fulfill their portion of the contract which was thrust upon them by the worshipers. There were, however, other occasions, when a slightly different set of considerations entered in. In a moment of battle it might not seem sufficient to propose the ordinary contract, and an attempt was sometimes made to compel the god's action by performing the promised return in advance, and thus placing the deity in the delicate position of having received something for which he ought properly to make return. This "binding" of the god was most frequently accomplished by what was known as a "devotio." The leader on one side offered up his life for the cause, and "devoted" himself as a human sacrifice to the gods of the world below by riding to his death into the ranks of the enemy. If his sacrifice was successful, — that is, if the enemy killed him, — the offering was supposed to exert an almost compulsory power over the action of the deity, and to secure the victory for those whose leader had thus given his life in their behalf. To carry this curious reasoning one step farther, we may remark that, if the enemy learned of this project, they had but to open their ranks and let the would-be human sacrifice pass through unharmed, in order to bring to naught the carefully laid plans of their adversaries.

In this scheme of things the function of the priest was that of the expert, the legal adviser. He had no especial advantages so far as the gods were concerned. They were no more interested in him than in any of the lay members of the community. He was, therefore, in no sense an intercessor between god and man. But he had given his attention to the study of the contracts between man and god, and above all he knew the name of the god who should be addressed in each particular circumstance. Thus it was expedient to consult him and gain the benefit of his knowledge.

These, therefore, were the conditions under which the religious life of the Romans began. The object of religion was to gain the assistance of the gods on behalf of the propagation of the race. These gods were unknown powers naked of almost every personal attribute. The relation of man to them was a scrupulous observance of forms, forms which had been handed down from the distant past, and whose custodians were the priests.

We must conceive of our early Romans as passing hundreds of years in the slow development of these concepts, living meanwhile in these little hilltop settlements, for Rome as a city did not yet exist. What would have become of these people, had they been left to themselves, we cannot say, for they were not left alone, and a great nation was already on the way to help them.

Great nations like great individuals are always mysterious, and no man has ever been able to explain satisfactorily the greatness of Rome. We feel her greatness, we see the results of it in action, but we cannot explain it, for its causes are hidden from us. In Rome's case, however, we can point out at least one obvious element of greatness, her willingness to learn of others. No nation was ever more ready to accept advice, to gain knowledge, to adopt ideas. When we stop to consider how much Rome learned from others, we are almost appalled. We are familiar with what Greece did for her in literature and art; we shall see later in these chapters what a vast amount the Orient gave her in religious matters. But we have never fully realized the contribution of Etruria. If we find that her political instincts and her governmental training came from the Etruscans, we may well ask, "What is there left that is really Roman?" The answer is not far to seek. Everything is left which was there at the beginning. The miracle of Rome was and is her ability to preserve her individuality, not as a thing apart laid up in a napkin, but to use it and by it to subdue all things unto herself. She did not necessarily always improve on that which was given her, but she always adapted it to herself. She always transfused it with her own individuality. This is not to detract from the glory of Rome. Properly understood, this point of view really increases her glory. Her essence lies not in material accomplishment, but in the possession of those forces which have enabled her to subdue all things. This is an infinitely more lofty possession than a merely specialized form of genius, which allowed the so-called original progress along only one or two lines. Bearing this in mind, we may go forward courageously to a discussion of the Etruscans and their influence upon Rome.

It is not many years since the Etruscan problem was a complete riddle. To have spoken of it at all would have seemed foolishness, to have used it to explain other things would have been little short of madness. Yet entirely apart from the difficulties of the language, there has been a steady progress toward the solution of the problem, and now that one or two scholars have had the courage to generalize and draw conclusions out of the mass of material, we find ourselves in the possession of a large amount of coördinated knowledge. There are several conclusions to which modern investigation has led us, and these conclusions seem practically certain.

It is clear that the Etruscans were a composite race, formed by the blending of those Italic people, who were settled in that part of Italy which we now call Etruria or Tuscany, with a race of invaders, who came doubtless out of the Orient and were probably of Oriental origin. They were, therefore, a mixed race, with all the advantages and disadvantages which often characterize that status, the quick sympathy, the wide outlook, the rapid accomplishment, offset by the sentimental diffusion of power, the lack of intensity, and the absence of permanence and continuity.

It has been further established that the invading portion of the mixed race did not enter Italy nearly as early as had been previously supposed. It used to be thought that they had come into Italy not long after the Italic invasion itself, perhaps eleven or twelve centuries before the birth of Christ. But there is now good reason to suppose that their entrance did not precede the year B.C. 800. The evidence is complicated, but it seems conclusive. Those who find it difficult to understand how, coming at this late day, they could have worked out their architectural development, should remember that they may have brought a very large portion of it with them. The long sepulchral chambers, with their false arching, which are found so frequently in the southern part of Etruria, bear very strong resemblance to the graves of Lydia; whereas the so-called "bee-hive" tombs are somewhat similar to the nauraghi of Sardinia. There seem to have been strong commercial relations between Sardinia and Etruria as early as the seventh century. One proof of the interchange of products is the frequent presence in Etruria of the boat-shaped vases which are peculiar to Sardinia. In all probability, therefore, the Etruscans entered Italy about the year B.C. 800, not so very long before the beginnings of Greek colonization in the south of Italy.

In the third place, it is clear that this invading race came from the Orient, and also that they came by sea, a splendid verification of Herodotus. Not only would the sea route be the natural course for a great seafaring people, but they have left traces of their passage behind them, both on the islands of the northern Ægean, especially Lemnos, Samothrace, Lesbos, and Imbros; and in Egypt; for though the famous inscription on Lemnos is of a much later date, i.e., the sixth century, the existence of Etruscans there at all would seem probable only in connection with their eastward journey. It must not be supposed, of course, that this journey from Asia Minor to Italy was undertaken *en masse* as a great maritime migration; it was rather the gradual westward movement of small parties, scattered over the coast line of Asia Minor. Their arrival on the coast of Italy would be, therefore, equally gradual, and the amalgamation with the native inhabitants all the more easy and natural.

Further, it has been shown that in coming out of the
Orient they tarried for a while under Greek influence in
Asia Minor. Their acquaintance with Greek myths is
too intimate to have been acquired second-hand and
merely through the medium of objects of art. They
must of necessity have spent some generations in a
Greek environment. Their very perversion of Greek
myths is a sign of their familiarity with them. The
myths had become, as it were by adoption, their own
personal property, and they unconsciously adapted
them to their own needs.

And lastly, we have the most interesting conclusion of
all, for it seems almost beyond a peradventure, that
their original home, or at least a very long abiding-place,
was Babylon. Every year, as our knowledge of Babylonian religion grows greater, we see stronger and
stronger resemblances. The characteristic feature of
Etruscan religion is the *haruspicina*, the art of divination by means of the examination of the entrails of the
victims, especially of the liver. Yet this is a purely
Babylonian method. It is true that the Greeks too
adopted it, but with them it does not precede the sixth
century; a time when the Etruscans had long passed out
of Greek territory. Then, too, the whole idea of the
templum or sacred rectangle in the sky, and its division
into regions, and the application of the whole to the
parts of the liver, are at once Etruscan and Babylonian.

These are the new and almost certain facts upon

which we may base our understanding of the origin of the
Etruscans. Regarding their rôle in the peninsula of
Italy we are also relatively well informed. Their power
and significance seem to have extended over a period
of about five hundred years, from B.C. 800 to B.C. 300,
but long after this latter date, and in fact even down into
the Empire, they exerted an influence upon Rome. They
seemed to have landed first on the southern part of the
Etruscan coast, near Veii, Tarquinii, etc., but they also
landed further north, at Cosa near Orbetello, and still
further north at Volaterræ. They were a seafaring people, and therefore in their new habitat they became a
city-loving people, like their much later successors, the
Lombards, the "Lords of Cities." But their cities were
at first simple affairs surrounded by a rampart of earth.
The stone walls, which were formerly thought to go
back into a very early period, are in no case older than
the end of the seventh century. They are a development of the Etruscans themselves, and are probably
contemporary with the more elaborate architecture of
their tombs. Even the walls of Volaterræ, which give
every appearance of a great age, must be younger than
the graves which they inclose, and hence do not ante-
date the end of the seventh century, which is about the
same time that stone walls appear in the Æolian and
Ionian cities of Asia Minor. Similarly in Italy itself the
walls of Norba, which seem so extremely old, date from
the end of the sixth or the beginning of the fifth century,

and the venerable fortifications of Alatri are not much
older.

Gradually the Etruscan power extended northeast-
ward and southward. In the one direction, they settled
at Fiesole, Perugia, then across the Apennines at Felsina (Bologna), and so up into the valley of the Po.
This settlement in the valley of the Po commences in
the last half of the sixth century. Of the famous league
of twelve Etruscan cities, which were founded there,
only three are known to us surely by name, Felsina (Bologna), Melpum, and Mantua. In the other, the southern, direction the Etruscans founded Volsinii (Orvieto)
about the end of the seventh century. No graves have
been found there which precede the year 600. It seems
likely, therefore, that this was an entirely new Etruscan foundation, and that there was no preceding Um-
brian town on the same site. It must have been at about
the same time that they conquered Falerii. Falerii they
found already established by the Umbrians. But they
captured it and gradually increased the city by absorb-
ing into it the settlements on the neighboring hilltops,
eventually surrounding the whole by a wall of stone.
This case is particularly interesting to us because, as we
shall see in a moment, virtually the same thing happened
in Rome. Thus the Etruscans descended into the plain
of Latium and thus they come into our story.

It is not likely that the capture of Rome was at the
time a notable event in their career. The group of settle-

ments, out of which they were to make a great city, was at that time of no especial importance. Here where Rome was to be, they found these more or less defenseless hilltop towns. They captured them and united them all into a city to which they gave the name Roma. One of the most interesting of recent discoveries regarding the Etruscans is the fact that this word Roma is itself of Etruscan origin, and is connected with the name of an Etruscan gens. Thus, though Romulus never existed, the gens Romulia did, and it was their name which was given to Rome. Thus Rome was born, Rome the city, as distinguished from the cluster of hilltop towns. But it was not alone in the name of the city that the Etruscan element has made itself at home in the vocabulary. The Tiber, so often called the *Tuscus amnis*, itself bears an Etruscan name, as do at least two of the old gates of the city: Porta Ratumenna, and Porta Capena; as well as the three old tribes, the Tities, the Ramnes, and the Luceres. Legend has preserved but scanty memorials of this founding of Rome. The four older kings of Rome are merely mythical personages, invented centuries after their time, but there may be a certain value in the tradition of the later kingdom, in so far as it recognizes the presence of the Etruscans in Rome, and gives us at least the one historical figure of Servius Tullius.

It was about the middle of the sixth century before Christ when the Etruscans founded Rome. The graveyard in the Forum corroborates this date, for, with the creation of a city, burial inside the wall and near the market-place would be impossible. In point of fact the latest graves actually date from about the middle of this sixth century.

Of the character of their conquest, whether peaceable or forcible, we have no knowledge, though the indications seem to point to a peaceable relationship between them and the original settlers. Eventually this power came to an end, but whether by revolution or by constitutional change we cannot say. The traditional date, B.C. 509, has only artificial value and is probably too early, while the story of the last Tarquin is pure legend, and the change from kings to consuls may have been an altogether peaceful one. It does not, however, suffice us to know the facts, we must allow them to take hold on our preconceived opinions: for most of us hold entirely false views concerning the power and influence of the Etruscans. The records which they have left behind them are chiefly works of art; and this art is characterized by such an extraordinary sensuality that we think of the Etruscans as a decadent people. But this is entirely wrong, and the reasons why we fall into this error are twofold. We fail to appreciate the Oriental element in the Etruscans. We make the common error of forgetting that what would be sensual in an Occidental is merely sensuous in an Oriental; and is in his case a sign neither of weakness nor of effeteness. Then, too, we fail to distinguish between the Etruscans of the sixth century

and those of the fourth. Yet there is a vast difference in
the type of Greek art which they preferred. When Tarquin or Servius Tullius, or whoever he was, founded the
city of Rome, the Etruscans were a strong and virile
people, and their influence upon Rome would be absolutely of the same character; and even though this
Etruscan culture was superficial, it was the product of
a certain amount of experience, and along with it went
a very high degree of efficiency and an extraordinary
power of organization.

Thus begins a marvelously interesting period in Rome's
development. It is a very curious fact that the Romans
themselves always frankly admitted their debt to
Etruria. Tradition made no attempt to conceal it; but
in spite of this the modern historians of Rome have
very largely underestimated the extent and character
of the Etruscan influence. Just as in the last half of the
nineteenth century, progress in Roman history was
made by emphasizing the distinction between Greece
and Rome, and, by eliminating the Greek elements, obtaining an idea of Rome before Greece influenced her;
thus in the twentieth century scholars are to take this
supposedly pure Roman product from which Greece has
been removed, and, analyzing it further into Italic and
Etruscan, to eliminate the Etruscan and thus arrive one
step farther back in the process.

The bald fact of the matter is this. We have in the
primitive Roman people, who are interested only in pas-

toral and agricultural life, a semicivilized people, whose
religion is at best only an advanced form of animism, and
whose religious instincts are concentrated in the conception of physical reproduction. There are visible only the
most rudimentary ideas of patriotic or political import.
And yet within a relatively short time these people come
forth into history filled with a stanch and invincible
sense of nationality. The religion of physical increase
has given place to the religion of patriotism. Now, when
we examine more closely, we see that all these political
ideas are centred in the cult of Jupiter Optimus Maximus
on the Capitoline — and yet this cult is demonstrably
Etruscan in origin. The inference is therefore inevitable.
The people who introduced this Jupiter cult have succeeded in arousing this patriotic instinct among the
Romans, and this instinct, true to its origin, as is the
nature of instincts, remained inseparably connected with
the cult in which it had its rise.

Let us look at this matter more in detail. When the
Etruscan wanderers girt the little hilltop towns with the
wall, and created a veritable city, they chose as their
citadel the Capitoline Hill, probably because it was
capable of being more strongly fortified than the other
hills of Rome. On this citadel they built their temple,
a temple to that holy trinity of Jupiter, Juno, and
Minerva — a trinity of which we have almost no trace
in Greece, but which is constantly seen in Etruscan art.
We are told that it was an Etruscan temple, and that

the Tuscan workmen who built it lived at the foot of the Capitoline in that street which was forever named after them, the Vicus Tuscus. Not only was the trinity a new idea to the Romans, but at least one of the three gods was an entire stranger, and had never before been worshiped publicly in Rome. This was the Goddess Minerva. Her original home seems to have been Falerii, that romantically situated town on the right side of the Tiber, whose modern name is Città Castellana. Worshiped there as the protectress of handicraft and the workingman, her cult seems to have wandered into Etruria. There, or even perhaps under Etruscan influence in Falerii itself, the trinity of Jupiter, Juno, and Minerva was formed, a trinity which was destined to become so typical of Rome that it was imitated in the capitolia of Italy, and in those of even the farthest provinces.

It is difficult to refrain from drawing a picture of those busy days in the new Rome, but the darkness is too intense and the danger of unbridled imagination too great. Yet we are not without gleams of light. One such friendly ray is the relation of the Etruscans to the Latin league. This venerable league, to which the hilltop towns of Rome well may have belonged, but of which they were certainly a very minor part, became at once an object of interest to the Etruscans. We do not know how long it took them to gain an important position in the councils of the league; but it cannot have been very

long, for the temple on the Alban Mount, whose foundations are still to be seen, was built at about the same time
and by the same people who constructed the temple on
the Capitoline. Thus we see Rome, led by the hand
of the Etruscans, beginning the conquest of Italy. The
power of the Etruscans in the affairs of the Latin league
seems to have grown apace, for it was not long before the
temple of Diana, which was to be a common meeting-
place for the league, was built on the Aventine. Diana
herself was in no wise related to either Etruscans or Romans. She was merely a wood goddess of fertility, who
was worshiped in the grove of Nemi. But this grove
was near Ariccia, and thus she was the great goddess of
Ariccia. When, therefore, in the course of time Ariccia
became an important factor in the Latin League, her
goddess became the goddess of the league. It was at this
time that the Etruscans proposed the temple on the
Aventine, and thus Diana came to Rome, where she was
to live an interesting and eventful life and later to become identified with Artemis.

In the building of the walls of Rome, the Etruscans
performed an act which was destined to be of great importance in the subsequent history of Rome. They built
not only a material wall of stone, but they drew first of
all a magic circle around the space where the city wall was
to be placed. This magic circle is called the *pomerium*.
It was in a sense the god wall, in so far as it served as a
defense against the foreign gods. None but the gods of

the state — that is, the Etruscan-Roman state — might be worshiped publicly inside this *pomerium*. Varro tells us that this drawing of the *pomerium* line was an essential feature of the Etruscan ritual of founding cities. He describes the ritual to us as it was probably preserved in his day and still practiced in the establishment of colonies in the provinces (*Lingua Latina*, v, 143): "They founded towns in Latium according to the Etruscan ritual; that is, with a bull and a cow yoked together, they drew a furrow in a circle, turning the sod toward the centre of the circle. This they did for religious reasons, on a favorable day, that they might be fortified by a trench and a wall. And the place from which they ploughed the dirt, they called the trench, and the clods themselves the wall."

This *pomerium* was to play a great rôle in subsequent Roman history. For centuries the theory was to be kept inviolate, and only the excitement of the Second Punic War was to lessen the sacredness so that certain Greek deities were admitted. But even then it existed as a barrier to certain Oriental cults until the time of Caracalla, when he, who gave Roman citizenship to the inhabitants of the provinces, gave also divine citizenship and a residence inside the city of Rome to the provincial gods.

No part of the physical wall of stone, which the Etruscans built, has been preserved to us, though some of the blocks which were in it may be found to-day in the so-called Servian wall. This so-called Servian Wall seems to have been built after the Gallic catastrophe (i.e., after B.C. 390). The real Servian Wall must have inclosed a much smaller space. For example, the false Servian Wall included the Aventine; which must have been outside the city wall in the days of the Etruscan domination. Those who are familiar with the traditional and current views of the foundation of Rome will realize that the view here adopted is entirely at variance with this tradition. The old idea posits the Palatine as the original source of Rome, and then traces the growth of the city by the gradual incorporation of the various other settlements, one after another. Entirely aside from the fact that the supposed antiquity of the Palatine dates from a relatively late period, when it began to be a popular and fashionable residence quarter of Rome, this whole theory of gradual incorporation is also of late origin, and palpably produced under the inspiration of Greek models, especially Athenian. The Palatine was doubtless one of the old hilltop settlements; but we have no means of dating these settlements one over against the other, nor have we any reason to suppose that any one of them at any time became, as it were, the mother-cell out of which the city grew.

The education which the Etruscans gave to the Romans did not stop with this new idea of the *pomerium*. They introduced to them their own developed system of surveying, especially in its application to augury. It is doubtless true that the Romans had long observed the flight of birds as a means of ascertaining the will of the gods, but the Etruscans taught them the additional refinement of, as it were, surveying the heavens and drawing certain imaginary lines, with relation to which the flight of birds would then be observed. Such a celestial quadrangle, or its terrestrial counterpart, drawn on the surface of the earth, is called a *templum;* and a building thus ritually inclosed is, strictly speaking, a temple. But this same idea of the quadrangle, divided in turn into various regions, is also applied to the liver of the animals slain in sacrifice, and thus arises the celebrated science of the *haruspicina.*

It is extremely interesting to note that, docile as the Romans seem to have been in relation to those things which the Etruscans were ready to teach them, they took very slowly to the idea of consulting the liver. Even to the latest times it was felt to be a foreign thing, and though in these later days its fascination was for that very reason great, the feeling of strangeness was never quite lost. Just as in our next chapter we shall see the Romans making use of a set of Greek oracles, especially in times of national peril, so on the occasion of terrifying prodigies, we find in Livy more and more frequent recurrence of the expression that the state "summoned haruspices from Etruria." On their own part the haruspices were clever enough to study Roman religion, in order that their science might be more skillfully adapted to the needs of the Romans, and in all their dealings they showed such a broad-minded religious tolerance that Varro (*Lingua Latina*, VII, 88) tells us, "the Haruspex ordains that each man should make the sacrifice according to his own custom." Then, too, the *haruspicina* was in many cases more convenient and in all cases more accurate than the observation of the flight of birds. Possibly the fact that the haruspex was, at least in later times, more of a specialist than the augur, may also have contributed to his exaltation.

Thus having received their primary education, the Romans were ready to rise in their might and cast away those who had taught them. For at a certain period of development such a reaction seems to be instinctive, and ought not to be attributed to a culpable lack of moral sense. We do not look for gratitude in the young. In Rome's case we do not know in exactly what form this reaction took place. To a certain extent it must have been the gradual growth of Rome's own self-consciousness. But the Etruscans, as a mixed race, may have paid the price of their ability by being early enfeebled. In any case the fact remains that, by the beginning of the second century before Christ, they had become merely an interesting survival; and the great mass of them had traveled out of Italy to the north into the Rhætian Alps, where the other Rome, the little town of Röm near Innsbruck, bears witness to their presence.

They had accomplished for Rome their appointed

work. They had raised her out of a semibarbarous condition, with a religious consciousness which saw no farther than the physical needs of existence, into at least the awakening realization of a patriotic purpose. Life no longer consisted merely in the multitude of the things which a man hath. This physical strength must be put to work and employed in the service of some useful purpose. This purpose was as yet undefined, but it was instinctively there. It was the creation of the Roman state. How transfixed these men would have been, had they been able to look ahead for a stretch of six hundred years and to see these beginnings develop into the great Roman Empire of Trajan's day, and then again for another stretch, this time for a thousand years, into the still more mysterious Holy Roman Empire.

But at the moment they, like all well-balanced persons, were engaged with the problem in hand. They were fighting their way to the possession of Latium, and they were becoming increasingly interested in a certain people in southern Italy. These people were the Greeks, and, thanks to the Etruscans, the Romans were now capable of at least a certain limited comprehension of them.

How they became acquainted with the Greeks, and what an extraordinary effect this acquaintance had upon their religious consciousness, will be the subject of our next chapter.

CHAPTER II

THERE are few subjects in the world in which divisions
and epochs seem so senseless as in this subject of ours
— the history of the religious life of the Romans. By
virtue of the fact that it is the story of a conscious
life, it is itself undivided and indivisible. There is
no break in the continuity of consciousness. We feel
perfectly sure that, had we been born at any period in
all these centuries, we should have lived our lives, the
great majority of us at least, without any sense of break
or even of remarkable change of any kind. But that is
true also of the life we are leading to-day. Few of us are
conscious of the really great changes which are taking
place in the religious life of this modern world. Yet the
historians of religion will some day mark an epoch and
draw a great line through the middle of our lives, and
our children's children will date a new period from these
present years of ours. Thus in the past we must make
our divisions, although the very visualizing of the
period causes us to feel that these divisions are untrue.

In the last chapter we tried to establish two successive stages in Rome's religious development: a primitive
stage in which the as yet untouched Italic stock was

concerned with the gods purely as the givers of physical and material goods, as the guardians of the herds and of the crops and of human increase. There was no purpose in this worship other than the mere instinct of social preservation. The individual had no spiritual life of his own, and therefore no individual religious interests. Then we chronicled a great change. This was not the coming of individualism. It was not yet time for that. It was rather the advent of a loftier purpose into the intellectual and spiritual consciousness of these people. In a word, we saw the coming of the Etruscans, their conquest of this region; and the great gift which their presence brought to the Roman people. When they came, they found a loosely united tribal community; when they departed, they left a nation behind them. There was something in the world bigger than the number of the sheep and the fullness of the granaries. There was a nation and a love of it. There was, in a word, patriotism, and a large background of religion to support it. Jupiter Optimus Maximus, Jupiter Victor, and his daughter Victoria, these were objects of worship which filled men with a new enthusiasm. Yet it was no new and strange thing soon to be lost. It was to be a permanent possession for at least a thousand years. It was to outlast as a vital power every form of religion then present. Thus filled with a patriotic zeal, possessed of an ethnic religion, the Roman people went forward into their history, whither we must now follow them.

It will be well, I think, to follow them for a moment in the purely surface facts with which we are all more or less familiar. We shall return later to the interpretation of these things. The development which we are now to discuss is virtually equivalent to the five hundred years of the Republic. The very fact that we are compelled to cover so much of human history in order to obtain the picture indicates how scanty our sources are, and yet I believe they are sufficient to justify our attempt.

The history of the Republic falls naturally into two divisions: the three centuries through the year B.C. 200 —in other words, through the close of the Second Punic War; and the last two centuries before Christ to the battle of Actium, B.C. 31. During the first of these periods Rome was fighting her way to world-wide supremacy. During the second, she was vainly striving to set her own house in order. We must treat of the two periods separately.

We begin with the three centuries B.C. 500 to B.C. 200. Of the first of these centuries we know but little; of the second more, but not very much; and of the third, a relatively large amount. So far as territorial development is concerned, the three centuries represent an enormous change. At the beginning, this city of ours was merely one member of a league of a few Latin towns; at the close, she was in possession of the whole of central and southern Italy, of Corsica, Sardinia, Sicily, and the two

Spains. At the beginning, she was an insignificant unknown community on the Tiber; at the close, she was the dominating force in the Mediterranean, and within another century all the western remains of Alexander's empire were to fall into her hands. Surely the inspiration of the Etruscans was having a marvelous effect and Jupiter Optimus Maximus was coming into his own.

Regarding these three centuries more closely, we see that the chief events in the life of the city were as follows. Sometime in the first half of the fifth century the constitution was changed from a kingdom into a republic. At about the same time, though not necessarily connected with it, came the driving out of the Etruscans, and the subsequent series of wars waged by the Romans against them. It was not, however, until the beginning of the fourth century, that the Etruscan power in this neighborhood was thoroughly broken. In B.C. 396, after a siege of ten years, the Etruscan town of Veii surrendered, and from that time on the ultimate victory of Rome was assured. But though her victory against the Etruscans was certain, trouble began in another quarter. The Gauls, who had entered Italy from the north, and settled in the valley of the Po, till now held in check by the Etruscans, descended upon Rome. They came along the Via Salaria and entered Rome at the point where successful invaders have almost always entered it. They sacked the city, and then

Rome set to work to repair her walls. Thus was that wall built, the remains of which we to-day wrongly call the Servian Wall. It was certainly built after B.C. 390, and probably before the middle of the century. This dating agrees admirably with the evidence which the wall itself gives. The fact that certain blocks in it seem to be older can be explained by supposing that they were taken either from an older wall on another site or from some old building. The older wall may have been that which the Etruscans built. During the rest of the century we have the gradual extension of Rome's power in Latium and southwards, and the closing decades of the century witnessed in the city itself the rise to power of Appius Claudius, who built the first aqueduct and the first great Roman road, the Via Appia. This road was to be of vital importance in Rome's subsequent history, until under the empire it had to yield the first place to the Via Flaminia, which Gaius Flaminius built some ninety years after the Via Appia.

The story of the third century is familiar to many of us. At its beginning, Rome fought with Pyrrhus for the control of southern Italy, Magna Græcia. Then came the desperate wars between Rome and her most powerful adversary, Carthage, ending in the struggle for existence against Hannibal.

This is a simple story in its outlines; we are all familiar with it, yet it really explains very little. If we rest content with it, we shall find ourselves entirely out of touch with the Romans as we meet them, let us say, in the days of Plautus and Terence. We shall have no fruitful knowledge of what was really happening. The people will remain mere puppets for us, and we shall not be able to enter into their lives. Such superficial historical knowledge is of very little value. Let us attempt, therefore, to make a really vital acquaintance with the people of these centuries. The underlying fact which explains the development of Rome during this period is the influence of Greece. When we think of what Greece herself was doing between B.C. 500 and B.C. 200, we are not surprised that her influence should have reached Italy. But we must not forget that, for the major portion of these three hundred years, it was not the motherland of Greece which was influencing Rome, but rather the colonies in southern Italy, especially the very early settlement at Cumæ. It is important to keep this distinction in mind, because much that happened later in Rome can best be explained by the fact that the source of her inspiration was an inferior one.

In estimating the influence of one nation upon another, modern parallels are of little value, because of the totally changed character of the processes of communication. In antiquity the first influence seems to have been purely commercial. But the importation of products required human agency, hence the commercial traveler. And these travelers, bringing their own gods with them, established the second kind of influence, that of religion and myth. Finally, much later, came the purely intellectual influence by the medium of literature.

In the case of the influence of Greece on Rome, the purely commercial stage was reached very early, even before the Etruscans came, for we find Greek vases from southern Italy in the graveyard in the Forum, which ceased to be used when the Etruscans conquered Rome. The influence of Greek religion and myth seems to have become prominent during the Etruscan domination. Doubtless the Etruscans themselves, with their love of Greek things, assisted materially in this. Finally, the influence of literature did not make itself felt until the middle of the third century, and does not concern us here. The vital factor in the changes of these centuries was the influence of Greek religion and myth.

The first Greek elements which came into Rome were, curiously enough, not recognized by the Romans as being Greek. There was, for example, the cult of Hercules, himself purely a Greek god, who came up with the merchants out of southern Italy, and in some way, which we do not understand, established himself at Tibur (Tivoli). Thence his cult spread to Rome, where he was received not as a Greek god, but as a god of Tibur, — i.e., a Latin-Sabine god, — and given an altar inside the *pomerium*, in the Forum Boarium. Then there were Castor and Pollux, who were the patrons of the cavalry in southern Italy, and came up into Latium, where they established themselves, especially at Tusculum. Thence

they, too, came into Rome as kindred and not foreign
gods, and received a temple in the Forum. So entirely
lacking was the feeling that these gods were foreigners,
that at a later day Hercules and Castor and Pollux were,
as it were, brought in again, this time under avowedly
Greek influence, given shrines outside the city, and
worshiped according to a new ritual, which differed
radically from the old-fashioned ceremonial of the Forum
and the Forum Boarium. But these were isolated cases.
The rank and file of Greek gods came into Rome in an
extraordinary way. As early as the sixth century, Rome
had established commercial relations with Cumæ. As
a result of these relations the cult of Apollo, the divine
physician, was introduced into Rome and given a sanctuary in the Campus Martius. In the train of Apollo
there came to Rome a collection of oracles written in
Greek. These oracles were the possession of the Roman
State. They were housed in the Capitoline Temple, and
placed under the guardianship of a newly formed priesthood. In time of peril the Senate caused the oracles to
be consulted, and the deities which they recommended
were thereupon introduced. In this fashion a host of
Greek gods entered Rome during the three centuries
with which we are dealing.

The earliest recorded use of the Sibylline Oracles is
in the case of the trinity, Demeter, Dionysos, and Kore,
who were introduced into Rome and given a temple,
in B.C. 493, outside the *pomerium*, near the spot where

later stood the Circus Maximus. These three Greek
deities were, however, given the names of three already
existing Roman gods, Ceres, Liber, Libera. The inevitable result of this identification was that the old Roman
gods were entirely forgotten, and the name came to
mean almost exclusively the new Græco-Roman deities.
But although 493 is the first recorded instance, we are
justified in supposing that the worship of Hermes, under
the name of Mercury, was also due to these oracles. Mercury received a temple in B.C. 495, also in the neighborhood of the Circus Maximus. It is only owing to the
fact that Livy omits to mention the circumstances under
which the temple was vowed that we have lost the definite statement that the cult was introduced after a
consultation of the Sibylline Oracles. But everything
connected with the cult indicates these Oracles as the
source of its introduction. In fact, the coming of Mercury and of the new Ceres are closely bound together,
and are the reflection in the world above of an interesting economic development which was taking place on
earth, namely, the introduction of Sicilian grain into
Rome, for Ceres and her companions represent the grain
itself, and Mercury the protection of the merchants at
whose instigation the importation was undertaken. It
was probably about the same time that the old Roman
Neptune, who had been primarily a god of water and
of rivers, but with no especial connection with the sea,
began to be identified with the Greek Poseidon, the

ruler of the ocean. By her worship of the deity of the
sea, Rome gained in a sense a control over the ocean,
and effected, as it were, a sort of marine insurance, which
was becoming essential to her on account of the grain
traffic with Sicily.

The Sibylline Oracles were doubtless used on many
occasions of which our records show no traces; and this
accounts in part for the fact that the next known date
of their use is B.C. 293, two hundred years later. It may
also be true that a reaction took place after the beginning of the fifth century and that the Oracles were not
used as frequently as at first, until the war with Pyrrhus
brought Rome into immediate and intimate contact with
Greece. However this may be, in B.C. 292, on the occasion of a severe pestilence in Rome, the Books were again
consulted, with the result that the worship of Æsculapius was introduced from Epidaurus. The snake, which
symbolized the god of healing and which the Roman
embassy brought back from Greece, elected to swim
ashore at the island of the Tiber; and accordingly it was
there that the sanctuary of Æsculapius was built. When
in the course of centuries paganism had given place to
Christianity, the work of healing, which had gone on
without change on this spot, was continued by the hos-
pital of San Bartolommeo down into the present day.
But this place of healing has not only the longest
unbroken record in our world to-day; it was also the
inspiration of that other St. Bartholemew's, which Lon-

don and the world know so well. Half a century later, in B.C. 249, during a critical period in the First Punic War, when Rome was terrified by a series of prodigies, the Oracles were again consulted, and Pluto and Persephone were brought into Rome and, under the name of Dis and Proserpina, given an altar in the Campus Martius. This was the beginning for Rome of those sæcular games which, two centuries later, were to be celebrated by Augustus and for which Horace wrote the *Carmen Sæculare*. It was at the old altar in the Campus Martius that the original inscriptions were discovered, which are now housed in the Terme Museum, and which form such an eloquent contemporary testimony to the event.

More important even than the introduction of these deities was the gradual diffusion of the religious ideas and myths of Greece. With amazing willingness and marvelous facility the Romans adapted all their old deities to these new ideas. Everywhere Greek parallels were sought for in things Roman, and a host of Greek legends were taken over bodily by the Romans with mere changes of names. Thus, for example, arose among the Romans the custom of attributing all innovations, including the foundation of cities, to some individual whose name was known. The application of this principle to the city of Rome produced the legend of Romulus as the founder. Thus the whole religious apparatus of early Rome was measured against Greek standards, and cut and altered to suit. In this process some of the old Roman deities, who had ceased to be vital, perished, so that only their names and the ritual of the cult remained, and they themselves became targets for etymological bowmen; while those gods who were still vital took on a new form and with it a new lease of life.

Such a relatively sudden reorganization of religious ideas could not fail to be dangerous even under the best of auspices. Conservatism suffered a temporary eclipse, and the loss of conservatism implied a loss of balance. But in addition to this, it so happened that the new ideas themselves could be only partially appreciated by the Romans, and that, like most ideas, they were very dangerous when only half understood. It is not wonderful that these busy practical Romans failed to understand the beauty of the religious ideas of the Greeks. No nation as such has ever understood them. At best a few individuals have succeeded in partially comprehending them. In view of all that the last decade has taught us about the origin of Greek art and its Oriental bearings, one is tempted to wonder whether Greece may not perhaps have represented the perfect equipoise of East and West, containing both elements in her intellectual as well as in her artistic life, an equipoise of which the world in our day stands in great need, but which it may take us some time to find. If such a theory of equipoise be true, it would account not only for Greek art but also for the Greek ideas of salvation by reason.

Be this as it may, the Greek idea of men as the sons of gods, with all the intercourse and companionship which such a descent implies, was something at once incomprehensible and terrible to the Roman mind. In their older days they had known nothing of the gods, those unseen gods who were known only in their activities. Then had come the tutelage of the Etruscans, who can scarcely have failed to impress upon the Romans something of that terror of the gods which Etruscan art so vividly portrays. And now the Oracles were here, and with them the fullness of the anthropomorphic conception. Thus there came into being that *superstitio*, that excess of belief, which was to be so characteristic of Roman religion from now until the end of the Republic, that Lucretius, in attacking it, thought that he had attacked religion.

This *superstitio* battened upon the crises and the perils of the Second Punic War, and it was in one of the darkest moments of that war that it received a visible incorporation in the introduction of the Great Mother of the Gods. Hannibal had been defeated, but he had taken refuge with his troops in the mountain fastnesses of southern Italy. It seemed impossible to drive him out of the peninsula. In her perplexity Rome had recourse to the Sibylline Books. There an oracle seemed to indicate that, if the Great Mother of the Gods were brought to Italy and worshiped in Rome, she would drive Hannibal out. The Romans, who at this time had scarcely heard of the Magna Mater, obediently sent for her, and in due course the meteoric stone, which incorporated her, was fetched from Pessinus in Phrygia, and brought by ship to the mouth of the Tiber. Livy tells us the story in full, and his account is worth quoting (Book XXIX).[1]

The oracle discovered by the Decemviri affected the Senate the more on this account, because the ambassadors, who had brought the gifts (vowed at the battle of Metaurus) to Delphi, reported that, when they were sacrificing to the Pythian Apollo, the omens were all favorable, and that the oracle had given response that a greater victory was at hand for the Roman people than that one from whose spoils they were then bringing gifts. And as a finishing touch to this same hope, they dwelt upon the prophetic opinion of Publius Scipio, regarding the end of the war, because he had asked for Africa as his province. And so in order that they might the more quickly obtain that victory, which promised itself to them by the omens and oracles of fate, they began to consider what means there were of bringing the goddess to Rome. As yet the Roman people had no states in alliance with them in Asia Minor; however, they remembered that formerly Æsculapius had been brought from Greece for the sake of the health of the people, though they had no alliance with Greece. They realized, too, that a friendship had been begun with King Attalus (of Pergamon) — and that Attalus would do what he could in behalf of the Roman people; and so they decided to send ambassadors to him — and they allotted them five ships-of-war, in order that they might approach in a fitting manner the countries which they desired to interest in their favor. Now, when the ambassadors were on their way to Asia, they disembarked at Delphi, and approaching the Oracle, asked what prospect it offered them and the Roman people of ac-

[1] I quote my own translation in *The Religion of Numa*, p. 96.

complishing the things, which they had been sent to do. It is said that the reply was that through King Attalus they would obtain what they sought, but that, when they brought the goddess to Rome, they should see to it that the best man in Rome should be on hand to receive her. Then they came to Pergamon, to the King (Attalus), and he received them graciously and led them to Pessinus in Phrygia, and he gave over to them the sacred stone, which the natives said was the Mother of the Gods, and bade them carry it to Rome. And Marcus Valerius Falto was sent ahead by the ambassadors, and he announced that the goddess was coming, and that the best man in the state must be sought out to receive her with due ceremony.

Again a little further on, Livy continues his account:

Then, too, the matter of the Idæan Mother must be attended to, for aside from the fact that Marcus Valerius, one of the ambassadors who had been sent ahead, had announced that she would soon be in Italy, there was also a fresh message that she was already at Tarracina. The Senate had to decide a very important matter, namely, who was the best man in the state, for every man in the state preferred a victory in such a contest as this to any commands or offices which the vote of the Senate or the people might give him. They decided that of all the good men in the state the best was Publius Scipio. . . . He then with all the matrons was ordered to go to Ostia to meet the goddess and to receive her from the ship, to carry her to land, and to give her over to the women to carry. After the ship came to the mouth of the Tiber, Scipio, going out in a small boat, as he had been commanded, received the goddess from the priests and carried her to land. And the noblest women in the land . . . received her . . . and they carried the goddess in their arms, taking turn about, while all Rome poured out to meet her, and incense burners were placed before the doors where she was carried by, and incense was burned in her honor. And thus praying, that she might enter willingly and propitiously into the city, they carried her into the temple of Victory, which is on the Palatine, on the day before the Nones of April (April 4). And this was a festal day, and the people in great numbers gave gifts to the goddess, and a banquet for the gods was held, and games were performed which were called Megalesia.

Thus brought in, she accomplished her work, and Hannibal returned to Carthage. But when Hannibal had gone, there remained in Italy a far worse enemy of Rome. It was the great Mother herself, with her cymbal-clashing eunuch priests; the first of the orgiastic Oriental cults, fraught with such danger to Rome, until they, too, became in time subdued to a more spiritual purpose. But for the moment Hannibal was gone, the Second Punic War was ended, and we turn to the last half of the Republic.

The last two centuries of the Republic present so many striking resemblances to the world of our own day; we feel so much more akin to the people of those days, so much nearer to them than to the dwellers in centuries numerically much nearer to ours, that a word of caution is necessary. The latest mode in the writing of history, in its desire to make the past live again, has sacrificed everything, that modern parallels might be exalted. This is, however, merely a reaction against the traditional method. Like most reactions, it is justified in its existence but it goes too far. If the study of the past is to be profitable, we must seek for differences rather than re-

semblances. This is not to deny the existence of many
practically unchanging characteristics in human nature,
nor is it to deny the usefulness of books which emphasize the resemblance of antiquity to the present, so as
to make the study of the classics more pleasing to the
modern boy. But those who have put away childish
things might derive greater profit from a treatise on the
same period in which differences were incisively characterized. We must of necessity follow this method, because these differences do exist and history does not
repeat itself. We assert this not so much by knowledge
as by faith. For the answer to the question, "Does
history repeat itself?" is the measure of a man's life.
If it does, then we are involved in the everlasting round
of Buddhistic thought; if it does not, then there is the
possibility of progress and the corresponding hope, and
our whole ethical life receives a new impulse. Realizing
these differences in spite of the resemblances, let us
now consider the last two centuries of the Republic.

Our task is more exactly from B.C. 201 to B.C. 31, —
from the close of the Second Punic War to the battle
of Actium. We must study first the surface facts. At
the close of the Second Punic War, Rome found herself
suddenly in the possession of world power. The possession of that power operated very largely as it does
to-day in producing a sudden commercial expansion.
The acquisition of power caused the formation of great
private fortunes. The upper, the senatorial class, amassed

wealth by the corrupt government of the provinces; while the middle class, the knights, grew rich by the process of farming the taxes. There were present certain primitive forms of combination in restraint of competition, but that which is most characteristic of the age is the primary importance which attaches to economic and financial conditions. There is perhaps nothing, in the whole history of the Republic, which strikes such a thoroughly modern note as the single fact that when Pompey was appointed against the Cilician pirates, instantly the Roman market experienced a fall in the price of grain. This market anticipation is thoroughly modern, and it may be questioned whether it would have been possible at any time between the late Republic or the early Empire and our own day.

The increase of private wealth brought with it, as it always does, the problem of investment. By the conditions of ancient life the field of investment was much more limited than it is to-day. There were no government securities to be purchased; for the government of Rome was a clearing-house rather than a bank. Her financial operations were in the main carried on for her by private organizations, which returned to her a certain stipulated sum, retaining for themselves the benefits of all further profits and the responsibility for all deficits. Further, there were possible no especial investments in the field of transportation. There was no such development of manufacturing that "industrials" entered into the calculation. Aside from unproductive articles of luxury, for which money might be spent, there remained only the purchase of land and of slaves, and the combination of the two in agriculture.

But these favorite investments were in their turn the cause of a wide-reaching social change. The small landowner, whose farm had suffered from the ravages of the Second Punic War, thus yielded to the temptation of selling his land or was forced into it by the foreclosing of mortgages. Deprived of his farm, there was no work left for him to do. He could not become the hired man, — the refuge which many of the farmers of America found under similar conditions, — for the presence of slave labor made this impossible, and even the steward or bailiff was himself a slave. Thus he gravitated toward the city. Arrived there, he increased the city population and created the problem of the unemployed. His one asset was his vote and his political support, his liability was the struggle for existence. These are the vital events of the seventy years between the Punic wars and the Gracchi. They are much more important than the conquest of new provinces or the building of basilicas in the Forum, — details into which we have no time to go.

And so we pass to our second period, the last century of the Republic. The outward facts in this period are relatively simple. A man tries to solve the problem of the unemployed, and to put the small farmer back on the land. To accomplish his ends he performs illegal acts and is killed. His brother ten years later takes up the same problem and becomes his avenger. To gain political control, he corrupts the masses by the first distribution of free corn. He subsequently proposes citizenship for the Italians, which loses him his popularity and eventually his life. Thus the Gracchi and the beginnings of socialism. Next arises a great military hero, Caius Marius, who makes good his lack of statesmanship by the strong right arm of the soldiery, a force which the Gracchi had lacked. Thus begins militarism. Then comes half a century of party struggle, devoid of principles and ideals, Marius against Sulla, Pompey against Cæsar. And finally Cæsar himself falls at the hands of the assassins.

These are not times in which we have a right to expect any growth of culture. There are two essentials for the increase of higher things: simplicity of life and the presence of lofty ideals. Both of these essentials were necessarily lacking in these years. Material goods were so distributed that those in the upper places were overwhelmed by the multitude of them, whereas the lower classes were deprived of those things which are essential to life itself even in its simplicity. Then, too, amid the rivalry of party strife there was no incentive to the cultivation of ideals. It was a generation of money and politics. It is not surprising, therefore, that the established religion fell into decay. In the first place, politics had no hesitation about entering into the priesthoods. There were, to be sure, certain priesthoods into which politics could not enter. For example, the "shadow king," the *rex sacrorum*, — that priest who, at the change from the Kingdom into the Republic, was appointed to carry on the priestly duties which in the old days the king himself had performed — was by the very nature of his position strictly prohibited from entering into politics. According to the Roman manner of thinking it was necessary that he should be appointed, because the Roman state had no right to alter the title of the person who from time immemorial had performed certain religious ceremonies. The change might not be agreeable to the powers above, and there was no legitimate means of ascertaining their opinion. Thus the "rex" was retained in name, but the danger of conspiracy against the republic was reduced to a minimum by compelling the holder of this position to stand apart from political life. For other reasons, the especial priests of Jupiter (*Flamen Dialis*), of Mars (*Flamen Martialis*), and of Quirinus (*Flamen Quirinalis*) were restricted in their public activity. But where politics could not go, there all interest ceased, and these priesthoods became of almost no importance, and in certain cases remained vacant for years on end. They afforded a sharp contrast to the three great political priesthoods: the Pontiffs, the Augurs, the Quindecemviri. These grew constantly in significance, especially since by the passage of the Domitian law (B.C.

104) they were thrown open to popular election. Persons thus chosen as priests would in the nature of things care for the political and not for the religious functions of their office. Thus the calendar, which was in the care of the priests, fell into confusion. Similarly the augurs, who were busy applying their science as an obstruction to unpopular political measures, cared not at all about the theory upon which their science rested. Thus the theory of augury was so forgotten that in Cicero's day two entirely opposite views were current. Then, too, the cult was neglected, and with the neglect of the cult, the ritual, which had been passed down by remembrance, was lost to memory. No longer were the temples repaired, but they fell a prey to the elements and the exuberant growth of vines and ivy. But perhaps most characteristic of all, because it touches most deeply personal life, was the abandonment of many private sacrifices. It was better to risk the wrath of ancestors in another world than the inconveniences of offspring in this. Thus childless marriages became the rule, and the sacrifices lapsed for lack of those who could carry them on.

But in looking at this picture we must not for a moment suppose that the community at large had no religious needs. Starve and crush it as they might, the religious sense was ever present with them. They could not kill it, but they could and did debase and pollute it. For the satisfaction of these depraved religious needs,

it was the sensational which was largely sought after.
The Great Mother had now received her own temple
on the Palatine, and her priests, with their clashing and
discordant music, were familiar figures in the streets of
Rome. The law still forbade Roman citizens to become
priests of Cybele, but evasions of the law were not unknown. When the Cimbri and the Teutones were threat-
ening Italy, the great High Priest of Cybele from Pessinus had come to Rome, and had addressed the people,
promising them the victory over the invaders. A Roman
official thought it his duty to interfere, and dragged the
speaker from the platform. A few days later this official
died of a fever, and Rome was not at loss for a reason.
The popularity of Battaces, the High Priest, increased
apace, and at his departure from the city a few days
later he was accompanied to the gates by a great multitude of men and women. The procession was not unlike
that of a hundred years before, when the ancestors of
these men and women had gone out of the gates to welcome the sacred image of the Great Mother, whose
High Priest had now deigned to visit them. Other gods
of the Orient were following in Cybele's train. There was
the bloodstained figure of the Cappadocian Mâ, whom
Rome had taken and identified with her own old-fashioned Bellona. Then in the days of Sulla there came
Isis and her priests.

The more exuberant forms of Greek philosophy became popular in Rome. Such crude ideas as those of

the Neopythagoreans, with their doctrine of the transmigration of souls, appealed strongly to their jaded senses. Even a pious fraud was perpetrated, and the so-called "Books of Numa" were said to have been found in a stone sarcophagus in Trastevere. But here the state stepped in, and destroyed the books before they had an appreciable effect. All through this period the action of the state is extremely interesting. Entirely apart from their own personal belief, the rulers of Rome felt it their patriotic duty to be the defenders of the state religion. They were entirely frank in their disbelief, and one of the greatest jurists of the day describes three kinds of religion: the religion of the philosophers, who explain the world according to their own doctrines; the religion of the poets, who use the paraphernalia of the gods on which to hang their myths and stories; and the religion of the statesmen, who defend the religious forms of the fathers because they are an integral part of the state. "It is expedient that there should be gods, and if it is expedient, let us believe that there are."

But these statesmen did not confine themselves to a mechanical accentuation of the past. On several occasions they carried on active operations against elements which they considered hostile to the public good. Again and again they expelled from Rome the teachers of philosophy. But their most dramatic act was the famous investigation of the Bacchanalian conspiracy in B.C. 186. We have the account in Livy in a series of graphic chap-

ters, and we have the dignified decision of the Senate
preserved to us in the original decree, in an inscription
found in Bruttii, and at present in the museum at
Vienna (C.I.L. X. 104). But the most significant feature of this decree is its broad-minded religious tolerance.
Bad as these societies of the worship of Bacchus seemed
to be, they were after all, in part at least, the expression
of religious feeling, and it might well happen that, even
after their condemnation by the Senate, a man might
feel that his duty demanded this particular form of worship. The opportunity must be left to him, though the
state might well hedge it about with all reasonable pre-
cautions. Thus the decree of the Senate ordained that if
any man felt it incumbent upon him to celebrate these
Bacchanalian rites, he should go to the city prætor at
Rome, and that the matter should then be referred to
the Senate at a meeting at which not less than one hundred Senators were present.

Toward the close of this period, in the age which
we call the age of Cicero, we have two very interesting
attempts to deal with the problems of religion. The two
attempts which we are to chronicle approached the subject from exactly opposite sides. In the one case, that
of Varro, the attempt is made to restore old Roman religion by learning; in the other case, that of Lucretius, religion is attacked and an attempt is made to destroy it.
It is very strange that the man who attempted to support religion accomplished nothing, while the man who

attacked it performed a distinctly religious task. Marcus Terentius Varro was at once a man of wide and exact learning, and an ardent adherent of the Stoic philosophy. It seemed to him a possible thing to exhibit ancient Roman religion as a revelation of the truths of Stoic philosophy in the form of parables. But he had also in view another purpose. The religion of the fathers had been neglected, and so largely forgotten. If it were to be restored, a knowledge of it must be regained. This was a primary necessity. And so he set to work in a series of books to write a systematic treatise on Roman theology, ritual, and church organization. The very pedantic character of what he wrote, the utter unpracticality of his theories, and the vagaries of his etymological speculation, are all of them proofs of his absolute sincerity. For these were all characteristics of Varro, and their presence in this book is evidence that he threw himself entirely into the writing of it. Then, too, there is the pathetic faith of the scholar toward the man of power, in his dedicating of the book to Julius Cæsar, in the latter's capacity as Pontifex Maximus. Of course nothing came of it; nothing could. The old religion was dead, and no one realized that more clearly than Julius Cæsar and his successor Augustus. But it was a labor of love, and as such it was not wholly lost. Even Augustine, who four hundred years later chose this book of Varro's as an exhibition of the vanities and follies of the old Roman religion, seems impressed with the spirit which breathed through it. For us the book is lost; we have only Augustine's quotations from it; but even from these quotations comes the perfume of the earnest ethical purpose of a Roman whose patriotism supplied the deficiencies of his faith.

Hardly a greater contrast could be found than that between Varro and Lucretius; and almost the only thing which unites them is their common interest in philosophy and religion. It is very easy to contrast them by saying that Varro used his philosophy to support religion, while Lucretius used his to attack it. This is also reasonable on the surface, for the doctrines of Varro's Stoicism were well calculated to support religion, while the doctrines of Lucretius's Epicureanism were equally well calculated to undermine it. The Stoic theory of the grand duality of creative powers — the father and the mother idea, the heaven and the earth — was peculiarly applicable to the older forms of Roman religious thought; whereas the materialistic and mechanical explanation of the atomic theory belonged to another world of thought.

And yet to stop here would be to convey an altogether wrong impression of Lucretius and his work. His attack upon religion was simply the result of his own intensely religious nature. His advocacy of the atomic theory is distinctly a religious expression. The world and the processes of existence are so wonderful if properly understood that he who contemplates them becomes filled with awe and reverence. There is no better example of this than the passage from the opening of the first book, in which he sounds the praise of Epicurus. I quote Munro's classic translation: —

When human life to view lay foully prostrate upon earth, crushed down under the weight of religion, who showed her head from the quarters of heaven with hideous aspect lowering upon mortals, a man of Greece ventured first to lift his mortal eyes to her face and first to withstand her to the face. Him neither story of gods nor thunderbolts nor heaven with threating roar could quell; they only chafed the more the eager course of his soul, filling him with desire to be the first to burst the fast bars of Nature's portals. Therefore, the living force of his soul gained the day: on he passed, far beyond the flaming walls of the world, and traversed throughout in mind and spirit the immeasurable universe ; whence he returns a conqueror to tell us what can, what cannot come into being ; in short, on what principle each thing has its powers defined, its deep-set boundary mark. Therefore religion is put under foot and trampled upon in turn; us his victory brings level with heaven.

Thus in his attacks upon current beliefs, in his criticisms of prayer and the ritual of worship, he is constantly unconsciously calling men to worship. Lucretius belongs in the category of the world's great religious mystics. At first sight he appears sadly out of place in his day and generation, and the object of his worship seems such a strange thing. And yet these contradictions are the best evidence of the genuineness of his mystical nature. He was born a religious mystic, one of the few religious mystics which the southland, with its absence of half

shadows and twilight, has ever produced. Neither the
banal trivialities of his contemporary Cicero, nor the
mathematical and physical austerity of the system by
which he chose to explain the world, could in any way
impede the outflow of his mysticism. He speaks with
all the ethical fervor of a great moral teacher. Take, for
example, the passage at the opening of the second
book: —

Nothing is more welcome than to hold the lofty and serene
positions, well fortified by the learning of the wise, from
which you may look down upon others and see them wandering all abroad and going astray in their search for the path
of life, see the contest among them of intellect, the rivalry of
birth, the striving night and day with surpassing effort to
struggle up to the summit of power and be masters of the world.
O miserable minds of men! O blinded breasts! in what darkness
of life and in how great dangers is passed this term of life,
whatever its duration! . . . For even as children are flurried
and dread all things in the thick darkness, thus we in the
daylight fear at times things not a whit more to be dreaded
than those which children shudder at in the dark and fancy
to be so. This terror, therefore, and darkness of mind must
be dispelled, not by the rays of the sun and glittering shafts
of day, but by the aspect and law of Nature.

Thus he points the way of salvation, but when we
start to follow him, we beat ourselves in vain against
the stone walls through which his spirit has passed.
Except in part in the person of Augustine, Rome offers
no parallel, and in modern philosophy we are reminded
only of the glass polisher of Amsterdam. For Spinoza

and Lucretius have very much in common, including their antipathy to the popular and established religion of the day.

We have tarried with Lucretius not only because he is a fascinating figure in himself, but because in a sense he is the best example of the one really great element of progress which had been accomplished during those long centuries of the Republic. This progress consisted in the slow and gradual rise of the individual. We began our chapter at the time when Rome was filled with the cheerful consciousness of her own nationality. We have seen the social instinct of religion gradually weakening in the presence of great material prosperity. Greece had given Rome new gods, but she had also destroyed the gods which Rome already possessed; and in their turn the Greek ideas had proved insufficient. Thoughtful men were turning away from the things which the world held dear; they were striking off into new paths of thought, all their own. Individualism was arising. With the development of that individualism, and with the problems which it in its turn created, we are to deal in the next chapter.

CHAPTER III

THE RELIGION OF THE EARLY EMPIRE: SALVATION BY REASON VERSUS SALVATION BY FAITH

OUR first two chapters have been in the nature of things more or less introductory. We have chronicled three periods through which Rome's religious consciousness passed, and at the close of the last chapter we found ourselves on the threshold of a fourth period. We have thus far traced religious consciousness from its birth as a purely social instinct, where a man's whole worship was directed towards influencing the gods in behalf of the propagation of the race, into a period where the purely social instinct turned into a national instinct, and where men prayed, not for physical increase in general, but for the progress and power of the nation. That was our first chapter. Then we saw the rise of the instinct of superstition. Whereas in the first two periods man had been conscious of his own strength, and had prayed to the gods rather that they might leave him alone and not prove hostile to him, because he felt himself confident to work out the problem alone if only he were not interfered with, in this new period, with the coming of Greek influence, and his own exhaustion after more or less severe contests, he feels the distinct need of the gods, not in a negative, but rather in a positive sense. He becomes conscious of his dependence upon them, and with this sense of dependence arises a feeling that he is subject to their caprice. The next step is quickly taken. If he is subject to their caprice, he must do what he can to win their favor. Hence arises the instinct of superstition. But in the presence of continued prosperity even this instinct of superstition grows dormant, and religious consciousness reaches its lowest ebb. It is then that the reaction sets in and the instinct of individualism begins.

These four instincts — the social, the national, the superstitious, and the individualistic — must not be thought of as succeeding one another in the way in which we have been compelled to portray them here. The characteristic of instincts is that they do not die, but are merely submerged. They still exist, and have a way of coming to the surface when we least expect them. We must realize, therefore, that in describing them one after the other, we are merely indicating the order in which they arose.

The political period, with which we are to deal today, is the first three centuries of the Empire, from the accession of Augustus to the death of Diocletian. We are to study the rise and development of individualism in religious thought. We are to see it starting from one point and working in two directions. The individual is to seek his salvation, either by reason and knowledge, or by faith and worship. Either the truth, which he knows, shall make him free; or his belief in the truth, which he does not know. These two tendencies are working side by side from the beginning of our period, and neither one precedes the other; but it so happens that the ideas of salvation by knowledge are more widespread and influential in the first two centuries of our period, that is, from Augustus through Marcus Aurelius; whereas the ideas of salvation by faith are more prominent in the last century. It will be well, therefore, to discuss, first, salvation by knowledge, and second, salvation by faith. But this matter of individualism is a very delicate one, and we can see its outline only by projecting it against the background. This background was the established religion of the Roman state. With it accordingly we must begin our study.

It was a boy of nineteen who was destined to take up the burden which Julius Cæsar had laid down. Listen to Augustus's own words regarding this crisis in his life. They are preserved to us in the brief "Official Statement" of his life activity, which he prepared a few months before his death.

When I was nineteen, I raised an army on my own responsibility and at my own expense. By means of this army I restored to liberty the Republic, which had been oppressed by the domination of a faction. In return for these things the Senate passed honorary decrees and added me to their number in the consulship of Pansa and Hirtius. And at the same time they gave me the privilege of a man of consular dignity, namely, that of expressing my opinion, and they also gave me the imperium. And they ordered me to see to it in my capacity of proprætor, together with the consuls, that the Republic should suffer no damage. Moreover, in that same year, in which both the consuls had been killed in battle, the people made me consul and also one of the three men appointed to restore the Republic. Those who had killed my father, them I drove into exile by legal enactment, punishing their deed. And afterwards, when they waged war against the Republic, I conquered them twice in a drawn battle.

From the beginning of his career until almost the close of it, the greatest strength of Augustus lay in his marvelous knowledge of human psychology. He was armed, not with the broadsword of military force, but rather with the rapier of diplomatic tact. As the world was then constituted, force could call forth only force; and he who took the sword would surely perish by the sword, and revolution would have been continuous, whereas the play of the rapier was after all in the nature of an exhibition. But one who really knows human nature recognizes the dominating part which religion always plays; and no really great statesman has ever been able to disregard it. In the case of Augustus it is no exaggeration to say that if we take religion in the old Roman sense, he was a great religious reformer. His purpose was doubtless to establish himself and his descendants upon the throne, but his outward activity was almost entirely directed to the awakening of a sentimental revival of the ideal of Roma Æterna. In his own consciousness there was no crass distinction between the end and the means. The establishment of his dynasty had come to mean to him the only salvation for his people. It was of course a theoretical error, as old as the world, and yet renewed every day, whereby a man feels himself appointed as the savior of his people. It was none the less a theoretical error, because, in the case of Augustus, he did actually accomplish a great good for the people.

With a quiet unobtrusiveness, which was characteristic of all that he did, Augustus set about the task of awakening in men's minds the long-forgotten chords of patriotism; and the instruments which he used to make this music were of such varied kinds that each man after his own fashion was compelled to hear. To those who were very deaf, indeed, architecture spoke in the reorganization of the city of Rome, in the splendid buildings of the Forum; the Palatine, and the Campus Martius; in the Basilica Julia, the temple of Mars Ultor, the Ara Pacis, and, most conspicuous of all, the glistening marble temple of Apollo on the Palatine. Others heard the voice of Rome in the recapture of the standards which Crassus had lost to the Parthians, an event of such supreme importance that it is portrayed on the centre of the breastplate in the famous statue of Augustus from Prima Porta. Still others heard the poets' song, — a Virgil, a Horace, a Tibullus, a Propertius; and when this dormant instinct of patriotism awaked, behold a reorganized state religion in which every man might join.

Under the new régime political life was bound to become atrophied, but the religious life opened wider and wider possibilities. We cannot here go into all the details of this reorganization. Idealist though he was, he built here as always upon a material foundation. The fall of the state religion had been caused to a large extent by the neglect of the priesthoods. Those priesthoods, such as the augurs and pontiffs, which had been filled with politicians, must be taught the seriousness of their religious functions; those which did not permit of politics, and had, therefore, been neglected, must be filled and kept filled, and the dignity and honor of the office must be its own reward. But if men were ever again to respect the gods, the places where the gods were worshiped must be restored and made worthy of respect. Hence the title which men gave him, "*Templorum omnium conditor ac restitutor*," and the long list of restorations in the *Monumentum Ancyranum:* "The temple of Apollo on the Palatine with its porticos, the temple of Divus Julius, the Lupercal, . . . the temples of Jupiter Feretrius and of Jupiter Tonans on the Capitoline, the temple of Quirinus, the temple of Minerva, the temple of Juno Regina, the temple of Jupiter Libertas on the Aventine, the temple of the Lares in 'summa sacra via,' the temple of the Penates in the Velia, the temple of Juventas, the temple of the Magna Mater on the Palatine I built . . . eighty-two temples of the gods in the city I in my sixth consulship rebuilt according to senatorial decree, no temple being omitted which at that time had need of repair."

But to arouse the enthusiasm of the masses more was needed than priests and temples. There must be the splendor of the cult as well. Hence such a performance as the Ludi Sæculares of B.C. 17, whose stone protocol we have preserved to us with its "*carmen composuit Q. Horatius Flaccus,*" and the poem, too, which Horace wrote has been saved for us.

Thus was laid a firm foundation of material things and old-fashioned ideas; and now Augustus was free to build upon it and to construct such new things as might serve his purpose. The building of the great white marble temple on the Palatine was doubtless the most conspicuous, but possibly the least fruitful of his innovations. After all, Apollo was the god whom Augustus himself chose to worship, and whatever influence the Palatine cult subsequently had was owing more to its material gorgeousness than to its spiritual appeal.

There was, however, another innovation which affected the people of Rome far more deeply. This was the reorganization of the worship of the Lares at the street corners. These shrines to the Lares Compitales, built at the crossing of the streets, had long been the centres of informal political clubs, clubs which Julius Cæsar, for example, had found so difficult to control that he had foolishly tried to suppress them.

With a magic touch, — tact in its literal sense, —

Augustus restored these clubs and gave them official recognition, with one slight change, which was to mean so much. Between the figures of the Lares was to stand from henceforth the "Genius" of Augustus, that old animistic concept of the divine parallel. Hereafter when these clubs met, they worshiped their Lares, and in addition the ideal of the emperor. Thus his divine parallel was present at all their deliberations. But lasting as was the hold thus obtained, it was circumscribed in its area and confined to the city of Rome.

Thus we turn to the most important religious institution in the Augustan scheme, the establishment of emperor worship. It cannot in any sense be affirmed that Augustus invented emperor-worship, nor is it true that he introduced it into Rome. It was in the world long before his day, and to a certain degree it had already entered Rome before he came to power. It is nevertheless strictly true that he controlled it and by very delicate manipulation, by processes of encouragement and discouragement, now by toleration and again by energetic prohibition, he shaped it and welded it into the instrument which it was to be in the subsequent history of the Empire. It is difficult for us to realize the power that emperor-worship possessed during the centuries to come. It was in a sense the only universal form of religion in the Roman Empire. We have, to be sure, inscriptions to Jupiter from all parts of Rome's territory, and his cult might seem as universal as that of the emperors. But this is an error. The name Jupiter in these inscriptions conceals a score of totally different deities, for in the nature of things the chief god of each region would readily be identified with Jupiter. But in the case of the emperor it was one and the same deity from Hadrian's Wall in Britain to the upper cataracts of the Nile, and from the Pillars of Hercules to the banks of the Euphrates. And when, in B.C. 29, Augustus dedicated the temple of Divus Julius in the Forum, on the spot where Cæsar's body had been burned, he was beginning the organization of the one great conservative force which was to hold the Empire together.

It is very interesting in this connection to observe that the form which emperor-worship took in the Roman Empire was one consonant with Western ideals, in a word, that the Oriental idea of the worship of the living emperor was changed into the worship of the dead emperor. The compromise was effected by permitting the worship of the Genius of the living emperor; and even in the latter days, when under Diocletian Oriental ideas had almost entirely conquered the West, and though the living emperor was to all practical intents and purposes worshiped, a regard for good form still held a thin veil of adjectives and abstract nouns between the physical person of the living emperor and the gaze of the worshiper.

And so Augustus died, and left his scheme of things to his successors to be tried out in the succeeding centuries. It is very wonderful how successful that scheme was and how capable of rational alteration; and it is surprising to what an extent it controlled the masses of the people in the two hundred years which followed. We have no need to pass through the outward political events of these years, for we have sufficient material at our disposal in the records of the inner life. We have gained our background, and we are now to trace the rise of individualism.

If one had spoken to a Roman in the fourth century, or even in the third century, before Christ, concerning his soul, its sinfulness, and its need of salvation, there would have been no discussion possible, for the person addressed would not have understood what it was all about. It is very difficult for us to put ourselves in such a position of innocence; but we can at least realize that there are certain Oriental nations of the present day who do not understand these concepts, who have indeed a sense of right and wrong, but who have not the consciousness of an individual soul, and hence can neither feel its guilt nor desire its salvation. The origin of this idea of the personal soul is obscured in great mystery. It was not present at the time of the Punic Wars. We see only scanty traces of it in the literature of the Ciceronian age, and yet in the time of Seneca it was absolutely prevalent. Various explanations may be suggested. The theory most commonly advanced is that these ideas were neurotic, that they are the characteristics of neurasthenia, and that so long as Rome was healthy and robust she knew nothing of these things. There is no question but that at the beginning of the Empire neurasthenia was prevalent among the upper classes. The slight value attached to human life and the ease of suicide are indications of this state of affairs. But we can scarcely conceive of the whole mass of the people as being neurotic, and yet this concept of the soul and its salvation is quite as common among the lower and the middle classes as among the upper ones. On the other hand, there can be little doubt that prosperity and luxury had tended to break down the strong racial instincts of more primitive times. Paradoxical as it may seem, there is much truth in the statement that self-indulgence may assist in giving birth to the concept of self. Certainly, too, the splitting-off and the differentiation from the mass are very much increased. But the essential thought is still lacking. We may obtain a soul, but how do we explain its sense of guilt? The only explanation which seems in any wise satisfactory is that these ideas were imported from the Orient partly through the doctrines of the later Greek philosophy, which was itself tinged with the Orient, partly through direct contact with the religions of the Orient. In other words, we have once again the spectacle of Rome owing a large debt to foreign influence. Such an individualism seems also the result of an excessive cosmopolitanism. Once given the idea of the brotherhood of man, with all the national boundaries removed, the ordinary man who is capable of an enthusiasm for his own country cannot rise to a love of the whole world, and thus reverts by reaction to the selfish individualistic standpoint. The teachings of a philosophy such as Stoicism and the universal ideas of Oriental religion tend alike to individualism.

But however these ideas may have arisen, they are everywhere present during these centuries of the Empire. Man is an individual, and as such has certain obligations and responsibilities toward the gods. These obligations are no longer primarily social; they are distinctly personal, and man is conscious that he has not fulfilled them. To add to the seriousness of the situation, not only is human life itself very short and uncertain, but the world itself is coming to an end. Must this individual self perish or is there a life beyond? Is this human soul capable of a life after death? And how can it purify itself so as to enter into that life?

These are the questions which men have put to themselves ever since, but which the Romans are now asking for the first time; and the answer is of extreme interest, because it is so particularly pagan and Greek. It comes to us out of that far-away Greek world, and though most of us do not believe it, there is always the chance that for the Greeks themselves it may have been true. Certainly it was not true for the Romans. The answer is: Sin is ignorance; to know the truth is to do it. Knowledge, therefore perfect knowledge, guarantees freedom from sin. The wise man is the holy man.

But if this be true, and if the world be soon to come to an end, then all knowledge is not equally profitable, but rather that knowledge which makes for righteousness; and if life be so short and uncertain, then the wise man will renounce the other things of life and give himself over to the better part. It is the new scale of valuation which the idea of the approaching end of the world brings with it. It is the gospel of renunciation. It is philosophy and the cure of souls, and its first and greatest spokesman is Seneca.

We may think what we will of Seneca's personal character; we may despise him as insincere and time-serving; we may even look on his death as mixed with melodrama; but we cannot honestly deny that he was a great power for good in the particular class of society to which he ministered. And "minister" is the correct word, for very few men ever gave themselves more unstintedly to the work of advising and helping their fellows. It is often peculiar advice that Seneca gives, but we must remember that his audience was very peculiar. His words often seem full of affectation, but we must remember that his age was even more full of *poseurs* than is our own. Thus he moved in his circle of aristocrats burdened with *ennui, bon viveurs* wearied by satiety, and *roues* who mistook exhaustion for repentance, and he preached to them all according to their need. He urged upon them self-examination and confession; and the reward which he set before them was that which they sought above all else, freedom from the terror of death. His methods were followed afterwards by many others. Those most familiar to us are Epictetus and Marcus Aurelius. It is an interesting movement, but one of relatively small dimensions; and we turn with a certain sense of relief from this philosophy of the salon and the boudoir to the philosophy of the market-place.

In many ages of the world the chosen few have sought salvation by knowledge, but it is only very rarely that the movement has extended to the masses. But the age of exclusiveness was giving way; salvation was not for the few but for the many; and if knowledge was salvation, then knowledge must be brought to the masses. And so the Cynic preachers and their kin began their missionary journeyings, until the bearded, unkempt philosopher, with his staff and his cloak, became one of the familiar figures of the crowded market-place and the lonely highroad. In this respect, at least, they were like the Franciscans of a later day — in that they were trying to distribute among the multitudes the bread that had been hitherto reserved for the masters. It was one of those moments, which come at great intervals in this world of ours, when those who have determine to share with those who have not. Sometimes it is knowledge that is given, sometimes spiritual help, sometimes food and lodging; but whether it be an Apollonius of Tyana and the bands of wandering Cynic philosophers, or whether it be Saint Francis and his brethren, or whether it be

General Booth and the Salvation Army, it all goes back to the same universal principle. In spite of the fact that for our knowledge of these Cynic preachers we are largely indebted to their satirist Lucian, the vision of them is by no means contemptible. They are not many of them really great men; they are given to rhetoric rather than reasoning; and they are quite capable of working pseudo-miracles in support of their claims; but there is a genuine earnestness about most of them, an enthusiasm and an absorption in their work, which in many cases raises them into the high circle of those who give their life for the good of their fellows. Even Lucian seems to feel something of this, and we suspect that below the sharp tongue of the satirist beats a heart that would find it easier to sympathize with them than with most of the other creatures of his day. And so, with some regret, we leave them standing on the temple steps or on the street corners, drawing a gradually increasing crowd around them, entertaining them and attracting them for a while, and then, when they have them in their control, teaching them of the Better Way.

It was not to be expected that the gospel of wisdom and of stoical perfection would appeal to the masses. It was help from without rather than from within that they were seeking. It was a power outside of themselves which was to save them, a power which would save them in spite of their own weakness. And their hold over this power, their control of it, depended not on knowledge but on faith. This power came to them in the guise of the deities of the Orient; there were a host of these deities but the differences between them were largely in externals. They had been creeping unobtrusively into Rome from the time of the Second Punic War, when the great Mother of the Gods reached Italy, but they did not attain to any great prominence until the third century. A brief consideration of this period will show the reason for their increase in power.

In our study of Roman history we are very apt to neglect the third century. From a superficial standpoint, it does not seem as important as the second century, when Rome's territorial expansion reached its extreme point; or as the fourth century, when Rome was visibly declining in prestige. And yet in many ways it is more important than either of those centuries, for it represents the interesting period of transition; and in this third century may be found implicit not only what happened in the fourth century, but also what happened in many of the succeeding centuries. For it is in a sense true that in this third century modern Europe arose. In it we see cosmopolitanism carried to its extreme. The brotherhood of the world, which the Stoic philosopher had long preached as an unattainable ideal, was realized at least in theory. For several generations before the beginning of the century the geographical centre of the Empire had moved from Rome eastwards. Those emperors who did their duty in fighting for Rome were of necessity absent from the city for long periods of time. The tendency, which reached its logical expression in the foundation of Constantinople at the beginning of the fourth century, was already in action. But this transfer to Constantinople would have been impossible had the way not been prepared for it by a certain act of Caracalla.

From the beginning Rome had safeguarded the privilege of citizenship; she had restricted it so that it attained and kept a very high value. "With a great price obtained I this freedom" tells one half of the story, and the proud answer, "But I was born free" tells the other. It is difficult for us to-day to realize the preciousness of this possession. Our modern world offers few parallels. In Rome the last wholesale admission of new citizens by legislation had occurred ninety years before the birth of Christ, and it was granted then only to put an end to a very dangerous war. But now, in the year 212, Caracalla extends Roman citizenship to the people of the provinces. There were several reasons for this action. In the first place, for generations the emperors had come from provincial families. Their interests in the provinces, therefore, were very strong. It was also an age when the jurists had great power, and universal citizenship was one of the jurists' ideals. But the controlling reason was one of economics. There were great financial advantages in this change.

But we are not so much interested in the change itself as in the results which followed from it. These were indeed curious. So long as Rome had stood apart from the provinces, the people of the provinces looked up to Rome as the ideal, and tried to imitate her ways as closely as possible. But now that they had all, as it were, become a part of Rome, the mystery was temporarily destroyed. Instead of imitating Rome, why should they not introduce their own ideas? Rome was no longer on the Tiber. It was everywhere where citizens were gathered together. Thus Rome ceased to be a geographical point and became a spiritual idea. In a subsequent chapter we shall see a still further development of these tendencies, when the city itself gradually regains its spiritual ascendency. But for the present the virtue of Rome had gone out of her.

It was the East which was attracting all the attention. The family of the Severi, who occupied the throne for the first third of this century, had come out of Syria; and still later came Aurelian, whose glory was the conquest of Palmyra and the capture of Zenobia; and in the closing years of the century reigned the Dalmatian peasant, Diocletian, whose favorite residence was Nicomedia. It was in every sense a triumph of the Orient, and it is therefore a period of peculiar interest to us to-day because we too are facing a grave Oriental problem. It was, however, at this time much more than a question of immigration and of commercial relations. It was the battle royal of Eastern versus Western thought, a battle which in a sense resulted in a compromise, the traces of which we can still see to-day.

To realize the power of Eastern ideas in Rome, we have but to recall the picture of the Emperor Elagabalus, and the meteoric symbol of El Gabal; we have but to remember the temple on the Palatine, whither Elagabalus sought to bring together all that was holiest in Rome, a pathetic catalogue, as the *Vita Elagabali* gives it: "And he consecrated El Gabal on the Palatine Hill, near the imperial palace, and he built him a temple, and he desired to bring into that temple the image of the Magna Mater and the fire of Vesta and the Palladium and the shields and all things that were sacred to the Romans; and he strove to bring it to pass that no god save El Gabal should be worshiped in Rome."

A half a century later, Aurelian built in the Campus Martius the great temple to his Sun-God, the *Deus Sol Invictus*, and at the close of the century, Diocletian, in a court which was entirely governed by Oriental etiquette, boasted that his power depended upon the favor of Mithras.

The secret of the fascination which the Orient exercised over Rome lay in its powerful appeal to the emotions. The idea that the world was coming to an end was to a large degree correct. The feeling, for example, of such a man as Marcus Aurelius, that he was living in an old and weary world, was much more than a mere reflex of neurasthenia. It was true that the world was old and weary, and that it was to end and to give place to a new order of things. Rome was experiencing an emotional old age. It was not calm and contemplative joy called forth by knowledge, but the delirious, emotional stimulus of the sensuous Orient that she craved.

And so we turn to the consideration of our problem, salvation by faith, and we find it in the religion of the Orient.

Under the old Roman régime it never would have occurred to any one to attempt to change a man's religion. A man was born into his religion, and so long as he lived a sane life he continued in it. His religion covered a very large surface. It concluded his duty toward his whole environment. He did not even think of himself as apart from this environment. His Ego was not lost in a larger social consciousness, for it had never as yet come into being. Religion was a social and therefore a national thing. Each nation had its own gods. If another nation's gods proved desirable, Rome might adopt those gods in case she succeeded in conquering that nation. But it was unheard of that any man should be interested in another man's religion to the extent of attempting to alter it.

But in the Orient religion had long passed out of this epoch and into the epoch of universality. Religion was not bounded by nationality. It belonged to the whole world, and was therefore the property of each individual. Thus by the very process of generalization it had become specific. But more than this, these Oriental religions posited the existence of the soul and acknowledged its sinfulness. That was the greatest impact of their appeal. They could purify from sin, and by this purification they held out the promise of immortality. Religion was not a matter of the nation, nor even of classes in society. In its presence all social distinction broke down. Men were all alike sinful individuals.

We can readily see the force of these ideas among the lower classes and, by psychological reaction, among the upper classes as well. But these were not the only appeals of the Orient. The character of their priesthoods had its effect. In Rome the priesthood had been an incidental thing, merely one element in a man's social and political life. But these priests of the Orient were given over entirely to religion. They had vowed their lives to it. It is the same appeal that the monastic orders made centuries later. We must not, however, think of these Oriental religions as appealing exclusively to the emotions. They made an intellectual appeal as well, for it was literally true that wise men had come out of the East, and the deepest learning of the day belonged to the Orient.

And last but not least, however varying the value which attached to their individual ethical doctrines may have been, the fact that these doctrines must be practiced, and that their religion required activity, introduced at once a moral element of a very high order. They were to be saved by faith, but their faith must be made manifest by works.

The Oriental deities who were present in Rome during this third century came in the main from four great regions: Phrygia, Egypt, Syria, Persia. They were very numerous, but not only did those from the same region have certain characteristics in common, but all of them, irrespective of their provenance, acquired gradually certain similar qualities. It is extremely interesting to observe that in every case there was a tendency whereby those doctrines, which had been originally physical and carnal, gradually took on a spiritual and religious character. For our purposes to-day it will suffice to choose three of these gods, one each from three of the four regions: the Magna Mater from Phrygia, Isis from Egypt, Mithras from Persia.

We have already chronicled the introduction of the Magna Mater in the time of the Second Punic War. It is important to observe that she came in as an authorized cult of the Roman state, a position of vantage which Isis reached with great difficulty and Mithras never at all. This was a decided advantage, and enabled her to offer shelter to many minor deities, who were never formally accepted by the State. In later times the characteristic feature of the cult of the Magna Mater was the *taurobolium*, the sacrifice of a bull in such a fashion that the worshiper, placing himself beneath the grating upon which the bull was slain, was bathed in the blood of the victim. We are here in the fortunate position of being able to trace the development of this idea. In its primitive significance the worshiper who drank of the blood of the sacrifice partook of the strength of the god, that is, of the bull. It is the ancient custom of "eating the god," the fundamental doctrine of the communion between god and man. We must rid ourselves of all ideas of symbolism. Man partook physically of the god, and so the god entered carnally into him. But in the course of time this crass idea suffered a change and became spiritualized. The bull became a symbol of the mystic bull, the author of creation and of resurrection. When a man descended into the trench, he died, went down into the grave, and was buried; and the blood which was shed was the blood of purification. Being purified, he was born into newness of life and came forth resurrected "in æternum renatus," "born again into eternity," an object of adoration to the assembled worshipers.

The Great Mother had the advantage of being early accepted by the Roman State. Isis and Osiris, whose cult seems to have been known in Rome as early as Sulla, fought their way with very great difficulty into official recognition. The Second Triumvirate decreed a temple to Isis, but the imbroglio of Antony and Cleopatra made the gods of Egypt so hateful to Rome that this temple was never built, and it was only after severe persecution that her cult was formally recognized by Caligula.

And yet these Egyptian gods had one great advantage. In the Serapeum at Alexandria they came under Greek influence and were thoroughly hellenized. Thence they came into Rome with the same preliminary advantage that the Magna Mater had had; and had it not been for Cleopatra, they would have received official recognition much earlier. The persecution in itself was of course a great assistance to their popularity, but an even greater cause of popularity was the ease with which they could be adapted to the current philosophical system, especially to the doctrines of what was known as Henotheism, the theory that after all there was but one god, and the multitude of gods were but various phases of this one god, various aspects of his being, called by various names.

The favor with which their cult was received is attested by the frequent references in literature, by a large body of inscriptions, and by a mass of votive offerings on the site of their temples near Santa Maria sopra Minerva. Here again we have another instance of the spiritualizing of the cult. The old Egyptian idea of purity was simply that of ceremonial purification, of the cleansing of the body. But gradually this physical idea became spiritual. The purification of the body was only symbolic of the purification of the soul. If the worshipers would purify their bodies in the service of Isis, Isis would herself purify their souls. Thus arose the idea of real chastity and the "nights sacred to Isis," with which the elegiac poet so often chides his mistress. Here, too,

there was abundant hope of immortality, harking back
to the oldest days of the Egyptian religion. The rise of
the idea of immortality is undatable in Egypt; and it
sometimes seems as if, in the climate which did so much
to preserve the body, the idea of the immortal life of the
soul suggested itself naturally.

But there was still another reason why Isis exerted
such a hold over the Roman people. The solemnity and
the dignity of the worship and the magic power of the
ritual were all akin to their own older ideas of religion.
It is no great strain on the imagination to picture the
daily services: the band of the faithful assembled before
dawn in the temple precincts; the solemn opening of the
sanctuary by the white-robed priests, the unveiling of
the sacred image, and the salutation of the dawn, as the
sun rose over the summit of the Sabine Hills, and filled
with gold the limpid air of the early Roman morning;
and then the second service, the farewell to the day,
as the sun was setting behind the Montes Vaticani; and
leaving painted in the sky the promise of the dawn of
yet another day.

But all these cults of the Orient fade into absolute in-
significance in comparison with that of Mithras. No
matter what a man's beliefs may be, the story of Mithras touches the depths of his being, not because of its
romantic interest, but because of its profoundly religious content; or perhaps we ought more truly to say,
because its religion is so thoroughly in accord with mod-

ern ideas. We cannot here trace in detail the story of the wandering of the god Mithras, out of the theology of India into that of Persia, out of Persia into Asia Minor, and out of Asia Minor into Rome; where his power grew, at first, with Pompey's Cilician pirates, then especially under the Flavians, and most of all at the end of the third century under Diocletian. It was not simply a religion; it was an atmosphere of Oriental ideas in religion, politics, science, and etiquette. It appealed so strongly to the court of Diocletian that the West stood in a graver danger of being conquered by Asia then than even at the hands of the Mohammedans, and yet the religion of Mithras never became an acknowledged religion of the Roman State.

As is but natural we know little of the mysteries themselves, with their hierarchy of worshipers. The initiated were divided into seven grades, whose names we know: CORAX; GRYPHUS (?); MILES; LEO; PERSES; HELIODROMUS; PATER. The first three grades were not admitted to the mysteries proper. To be admitted there, one must have passed beyond Miles into Leo. Those who had attained the seventh grade, PATER, occupied as Father a position of superiority over all the other six grades, whose members were known as Fratres, or Brethren. The transition from one grade to another was effected by picturesque and terrifying ordeals of initiation. Of the ceremonies of worship we know little, and such little as we know is derived from chance references, especially among the Church Fathers, and from a study of the places where the worship occurred. These places of worship are characterized by two peculiarities; they are always subterranean, at first in natural caves and then in artificial ones, and in the case of private chapels at least, in the cellar of the house; and they were limited in size so that not more than one hundred worshipers could be accommodated in one cave. When the number of the faithful outgrew the capacity of the cave, another cave was prepared alongside of it. Thus at Heddernheim, in Germany, we find three caves; at Carnuntum, four; at Ostia, five. The interior arrangement of the caves is generally the same. Along each of the long sides runs a *podium*, doubtless intended to accommodate the worshipers in a kneeling position. At the upper end of the cave stood the altars, and between them on the rear wall the relief of Mithras slaying the bull.

Of the theological doctrines of Mithras we know but little, and that in a somewhat confused way, when we try to fit together the representations in the monuments and the references of the Christian controversialists, who were of course its enemies.

Mithras himself is represented as born from a rock at the dawn of the day, while shepherds look on in adoration. His struggles and trials are pictured, and especially his slaying of the bull. This he does against his own will, to give immortality to mankind and to redeem them from death.

In the cult itself we know that there was a form of baptism, and a sacrificial meal, and that there was a ceremony of the blood that was shed for all (*mana cunctis*). They believed also in the immortality of the soul, in the resurrection of the dead, in a place of future punishments and rewards, and in the ascent of Mithras on high. In the nature of things, the Christians asserted that these doctrines had been stolen from them by the demons and revealed to these worshipers of Mithras; and similar accusations seem to have been made by the followers of Mithras. In both cases they were doubtless wrong. It is merely an instance of similar ideas arising under similar circumstances. Thus the whole Roman Empire was girt about by the love of Mithras, and we find the caves which served as churches in almost every province. Spreading at almost the same time as Christianity, it had by the middle of the third century outrun it in numbers and influence.

Never in the history of the world has there been a more effective organization of missionary endeavor, than in the ranks of the worshipers of Mithras. Their strength lay in the fact that they were all volunteers, who spoke out of the fullness of their own devotion, and carried their love of Mithras into the ordinary walks of life, where they were employed in the usual activities of the working world. They were at first either slaves or soldiers — and thus in both cases their missionary journeys were made, as it were, at the expense of others.

In many cases the slaves had been soldiers, who had been taken prisoners in war. Among the soldiers themselves there were of course the legions recruited from the East, many of whose members were followers of Mithras. But even more important, so far as missionary work is concerned, were the centurions, who, by virtue of the fact that they were frequently transferred from one legion to another, carried the news of Mithras around the whole circle of the frontier. From the mouth of the Danube to Hadrian's Wall in Britain, from Hadrian's Wall to the Pillars of Hercules, and from the Pillars of Hercules to the Desert of Sahara, monuments of Mithras are found. These memorials are abundant in Moesia; in Dacia scarcely a town is without them; and they are found in great numbers in Pannonia and Noricum. Germany precedes even the Danube provinces in the number and the quality of its monuments. Even on the seacoast at Boulogne, Oriental sailors from the British fleet had brought the good tidings. Mithras was worshiped throughout Britain, including London, York, and Wales. But we must not fall into the easy error of supposing that it was only a soldiers' religion and confined to the frontier. It spread through the interior of the Empire as well, carried there at first by the slaves. It was so well known in Rome that we have about two hundred inscriptions and monumental reliefs, besides several Mithraic chapels. At Ostia there are no less than five sanctuaries, and remains are found at Naples, Pisa,

Palermo, Syracuse; and even the small hill-towns — e.g., Spoleto, Sentino — contain Mithraic inscriptions; while southern France, especially Lyons, seems to have been a strong centre of the cult.

Nor was it simply a religion of under-officers, common soldiers, and slaves, even though they were its earliest devotees. The freed slave and the veteran soldier both became in many cases important persons, and the social success which they themselves sometimes failed to obtain, was very often reached by their children after them. Thus the doctrines of Mithras, like those of Christianity, grew up out of the masses and reached the Palace of the Cæsars. There Mithras, the especial guardian of rulers, could not fail of an appeal, and from Commodus through Diocletian his popularity was ever on the increase. With imperial favor came further popularity at the hands of literary men and philosophers. One of the greatest secrets of its growth was its ability to adapt itself to circumstances. Its docrines were sufficiently elastic to permit of far-reaching processes of accommodation.

Coming out of the Orient, and bringing with it the Oriental contempt for woman, it was par excellence a man's religion. But it soon discovered that in the Western world this was an insurmountable difficulty, and that Romans wished to share their religion with their wives and daughters; and that in many cases in the final analysis women were more interested than men in the things of religion. But this obstacle was easily removed by an alliance with the Magna Mater, which on its part was quite as open to women as to men. This alliance was also of service to Mithras in another respect, because the Magna Mater was a state cult, and hence by uniting with her, the worship of Mithras, which was never formally accepted by the state, received a certain reflected light of legal authorization. It was also owing to this alliance that the custom of the *taurobolium* was associated with Mithras. As we saw above, this was originally peculiar to the cult of the Magna Mater; but the association of the two cults, and the fact that Mithras is so often represented as slaying the bull, have given rise to the popular misconception that the *taurobolium* was an original part of Mithras worship.

We can scarcely forbear to speculate as to what the world would have been to-day had Mithras prevailed. What effect would his presence have had upon the progress of science? And what would have been the evolution of governmental institutions, had Mithras, the guardian of kings, retained his power?

And finally, what was Mithras? Wherein did his undoubted power lie? He was not the chief god of the theological system. That was Ahura-Mazda, who was forever fighting Ahriman. In the physical world this was the struggle of light and darkness, in the spiritual world the struggle of good and evil. The task of Mithras was to guard Ahura-Mazda. Mithras was the god of light, with a thousand ears, and ten thousand eyes. And so he became the god of truth and of oaths, and the great leader against the powers of darkness. His was above all things a militant religion. Life itself was one long battle, and the powers of light must fight forever against the powers of darkness. Every day was a repetition of the conflict. It was Mithras who made the dawn and drove away the darkness before the coming of the sun. It was Mithras who conquered at noonday. It was Mithras again who fought against the gathering darkness, and it was Mithras who caused the stars to shine in the night. But this was only a part of his work. It was Mithras who brought light and purity into men's minds, who drove away evil thoughts and temptations, and filled the spirit of man with a divine light. He it was who taught men the love of truth, and the great truth of the brotherhood of man.

CHAPTER IV

CONSTANTINE AND CHRISTIANITY

THE age in which we live is perhaps more deeply and intelligently interested in religion than any age which the world has ever seen. Among intellectual people to-day an interest in religion is almost universal; not necessarily an interest in any specific form of religion, but an interest in religion itself. The age of scientific materialism is past. Scientists are fully aware of the limitations of their field; while philosophers go one step farther and acknowledge the reality of the psychological impulse to religion. The religious instinct has been adjudged normal. Only two years ago we celebrated the centenary of the birth of Darwin. In that century the philosophy of history has made almost a complete revolution. Receiving a stupendous impulse from the idea of evolution, it quickly reformed all its methods and results. Then the inevitable happened; and the outward imitation of the natural sciences was followed by an inner imitation. Men began to talk about the biology of history, and to subject it to the laws of biological evolution. But now in these latter days the falseness of this method has been clearly shown; and history takes farewell of biology and allows her to go alone along her more intimate paths. All this has been accomplished in less than a century.

Our psychological experiment has been at least in so far successful, that we have found our religious instinct responding under circumstances which might readily have surprised us. It was not difficult for any of us, I venture to say, to enter into a sympathetic appreciation of the cult of Mithras. Many of us could enter also into the religion of patriotism; some of us could follow it even in its specific form of emperor-worship; and doubtless there were a few who found a certain satisfaction in primitive nature cults. This is not of our making. The old instincts are all there; they are being awakened anew. This reawakening has been to a certain extent the purpose of our work.

There remains but one thing, to connect the past with the present. This is our hardest task. We all of us found it easy to take a languid and patronizing interest in these pagan ideas; but even when we are brought to the consciousness of the fact, that these so-called pagan ideas were the forerunners of Christianity, and that, whatever our beliefs as to the origin of Christianity may be, it is our duty to fit Christianity into the framework of our history, we sometimes fear the consequences.

But taking advantage of the momentum which we have gained, we shall not find this difficult. In all the centuries of our work hitherto we have seen the continuity of a genuine ever-present religious need; and we have observed also the continuity of a genuine ever-present religious supply. But now, when we turn to the consideration of that religion which has continued at least in name up to the present, there is a danger lest we cease to discuss religion and confine ourselves to Christianity.

Probably very many different attitudes are represented among those who read these pages. To a large extent we agree in the facts, but we differ in the inferences. That is, however, the least of our difficulties. Each of us has the right to his own individual interpretation. The most real obstacle which lies in our path is our great difficulty in being objective. We are timid because we feel that we are dealing with a tremendous reality. Yet we have all this time been dealing with tremendous realities. We are not stepping to-day from the region of fairy stories into that of real life. The *taurobolium* of the Magna Mater was at the time and to the individual just as vital as extreme unction.

Then, too, this almost morbid sense of the ultra-seriousness of our problem affects us in the reverse way. Our objectivity toward Mithras enables us to see the beauty and the impressiveness of his worship. We become deeply interested in him. We long to know more of his mysteries and his ethical teachings. And yet the early history of Christianity is if anything more interesting and more picturesque than that of Mithras. But we shall surely fail to appreciate this picturesqueness unless we look at it with a sufficient objectiveness to become really interested in it.

If we can once compel ourselves to look at Christianity as a section of religious history, — the final, the ultimate, if you will, — the whole atmosphere of our views of both God and man will be clarified; and in the long run our respect for Christianity will be increased rather than decreased. I would wish it, however, clearly understood that in this discussion we are of course limited to the observation of the historical phenomena. We have no right to speak of anything concerning the other, the metaphysical side of our picture, and yet by this silence I would not have it understood, either that I am myself, or that I would wish you, to be oblivious of those other forces, whose existence may so easily be posited. Only we must remember that if we posit them here, we must posit them also in the whole history of religion.

Let us begin our work by a brief outline of the historical origin of Christianity. That origin takes us to the eastern part of the Empire, to the small tributary kingdom of Judæa. We are interested in Judæa, not only because the Founder of Christianity was born there, but because he came of the race of Judæa, and because he taught that his revelation was the fulfillment of the doctrines which were contained in the religion of Judæa. We shall do well to begin, therefore, with the history of Judæa.

By a slow development, which covered centuries, a collection of small tribes was amalgamated into a kingdom. This kingdom had its religious centre at Jerusalem, the temple being its natural sanctuary. Theirs was a purely national religion, and there was nothing exceptional in their deep-rooted conviction that they were a peculiar and a chosen people. There was, however, something distinctly individual in their eventual worship of One God only, who was not only their one god, but was the only true god, all others being at best mere idols or demons. This is quite a different attitude from the Roman idea of Jupiter Optimus Maximus, who, while distinctly the best god in the world, was by no means the only one. To this exalted form of the concept of god is owing the supreme confidence of this nation in its destiny as the people chosen of God, a confidence which, still existing in the faithful of their race, is perhaps the most impressive religious phenomenon of the present day.

In the year B.C. 590 the hosts of the Assyrians and the Chaldæans captured this Jewish kingdom, destroyed the temple at Jerusalem, and carried the people away captive. They were subsequently released when the Persians conquered the Chaldæans and captured the city of Babylon. The Jews were well treated and allowed to settle again at Jerusalem. Thus they lived under the Ptolemies and the Seleucidæ with a very considerable degree of liberty, though with no rights as a nation. They finally gained their freedom and became again a nation after a successful insurrection against Antiochus Epiphanes, who had vainly imagined that they would submit to Hellenization. For a century they were ruled by their own kings, until, in B.C. 63, Pompey captured Jerusalem, and twenty-three years later (B.C. 40) Antony established Herod the Great on the throne. Herod died in B.C. 4, and it is with him that the story of Christianity begins.

The life of the Founder of Christianity does not concern us here except to remark, in passing, that all attempts to deny his historical existence — and some such attempt is made every few years — are absolutely futile. The proofs are far more abundant than we would have a right to expect, considering how often undoubtedly genuine historical characters are so meagrely authenticated. His death at Jerusalem is recounted for us quite objectively in the famous passage of Tacitus (*Annals*, XV, 44), which is above suspicion. The historian is speaking of Nero's attempts to escape the charge, that he had himself set fire to the city of Rome, by accusing "those who, hated on account of their evil deeds, are commonly called Christians. The author of this name, Christ, was put to death in the reign of the Emperor Tiberius by the Procurator Pontius Pilate; this baleful superstition, repressed for the moment, burst out again, not only throughout Judæa, where this evil had originated, but also throughout the city, where all things evil or shameful flow together from all sides and are the objects of worship."

We are here primarily interested in the propagation of these doctrines. The success of this propagation was dependent upon several elements. These elements are not peculiar to Christianity, and they were being contemporaneously used by other religions. The first was the existence of the Roman Empire itself. The organization of this Empire guaranteed peace over at least a large portion of its surface; and the fabric of Roman roads, which was already several centuries old, made communication relatively rapid and easy. But these are, after all, merely material considerations. Be the peace never so great, and be the roads never so smooth, the appeal of a religion depends in the last case upon the attitude of mind of those to whom it is presented. Here Christianity had the same advantages as the other Oriental cults. The way had been prepared for her as for them. She profited by the same awakened sense of the individual soul and its sinfulness, by the same philosophical ideas of the unity of God, and that the many gods of polytheism were in the last analysis merely many phases of the one divine power. She, too, had found men convinced that the world was soon to come to an end, and that the most important work of man was the purification of the soul so that it might be worthy of immortality. There were absolutely no exceptional conditions created for the benefit of Christianity. It entered into the struggle of human thought with no superiority except what it contained within itself. In fact, one of the most tangible proofs of the beauty of its original doctrines, of the sublimity of the moral teaching of Him who spake as never man spake, is to be found in the workings of these pre-conditions, which not only helped but also hindered her, while they seem to have been only of help to her rivals. The organization of the Empire rendered possible organized persecution; philosophy created heresies; and the other Oriental religions, which in the main supported rather than opposed one another, ranged themselves unitedly against her.

Let us consider now in some detail the history of her progress. A band of Jews in the far-away province of Judæa believed that they had found the Messiah. The message spread quickly among a community, whose spiritual eyes had long been gazing into the distance looking for the Messiah. Among these Jews there could be no indifference to this message. Either it was a wonderful truth or a blasphemous falsehood. Thus the community was divided against itself, the one part telling the glad tidings of great joy, the other part horrified and scandalized at the enormity of the assertion. It is no wonder, therefore, that after his bold speech Stephen was stoned to death by those Jews who did not believe, and became thus the first in the long ranks of those who sealed their belief by their death. It is equally natural that a young man of excellent education, and brilliant intellectual ability, who was not only a Jew, but a Roman citizen, should throw himself with all the activity of his nature into an attempt to destroy this repulsive doctrine. The conversion of Saul of Tarsus and the rise of Paul the Apostle are entirely in accord with the most approved psychology, and may be considered as historical facts, so far as the phenomena are concerned. All these events occurred in the fourth decade of the first century. Gradually a church was founded at Antioch, where the followers of this new religion first received their name of "Christians." Then came the first great dispute. The Founder of Christianity had said to the woman of Samaria, "Salvation is of the Jews," and there was no doubt of that in the minds of all his followers. In fact, during the first years these followers were all of them Jews. But by degrees men who were not of the circumcision, became interested in the movement, and the question arose for decision: salvation is indeed of the Jews, but granted that as its origin, is it only for the Jews as well as of them, or is it for the Gentiles as well?

It was Paul, the Apostle to the Gentiles, who answered this question, and all the history of Western civilization waited on his answer. It is the fashion of our day to speak slightingly of Paul. Many of those who pride themselves upon their superior intelligence refer to him as though he had distorted the teachings of the Founder of Christianity. They would eliminate him and his work from our concept of Christianity. They would establish a form of religion purified of a dogmatic and legal theology. It is not proper that we should enter upon these discussions here. Our work is that of the historian and not of the theologian. But it is necessary to refer to this movement, because many of those who are interested in it fail to do justice to history. It may be well enough to stand in the twentieth century, and, disapproving of Paul's interpretation, try to eliminate it from our modern Christianity, but the moment this disapproval takes the form of belittling the man Paul, whose work in history they disapprove of, the historian must step forward to protest against the iniquity of the injustice thus accomplished. Christianity, itself of Oriental origin, so far as the phenomena are concerned, was translated into terms of the Occident by the very great genius of Paul. We may or may not approve of his attitude, but whether we approve or not, we ought not to forget, not only that the existence of Christianity in the Western world depended upon its being occidentalized, but also that in a sense the preservation of Western civilization depended upon this occidentalization. In things religious Rome had entirely submitted to the Orient; it was Paul who saved Western civilization by transmuting an Oriental worship into terms of Roman law. This he could and did do, because he was more essentially Roman than Hebrew. In these modern days of sympathy with the Orient, and desire to come into relations of mutual understanding with her, we may for a moment regret that Paul, in a sense, inserted the edge of the wedge which was to cleave East and West asunder and hold them so for two millenniums, but we should not forget how the

West has worked out its own salvation, and by progress in self-government has brought individual freedom into existence. This precious result could have been obtained only by the West alone unhampered by the East. Now that it has been obtained, we can calmly discuss a sympathetic relation with the East.

But even after the broad platform of Occidentalism had been laid down by Paul, for a long time all the converts to Christianity were thoroughly acquainted with the Jewish tradition and the Jewish law. Gradually, however, the difference between Judaism and Christianity grew wider. This was the inevitable consequence of their directly opposing points of view: those who were still looking for the Messiah and keeping the old law, and those who had found the Messiah and were therefore no longer under the law.

Meantime the new doctrines had reached the city of Rome, where of course the inevitable confusion between Jews and Christians was the order of the day. The Jewish population of Rome had increased very largely after Pompey's capture of Jerusalem. The city was full of Jewish slaves and freedmen, who lived, most of them, across the river in Trastevere. There were so many Jews in Rome that, in A.D. 19, Tiberius sent four thousand of them to fight in Sardinia. But the first traces of Christians among the Jews are found in connection with the expulsion carried out by the Emperor Claudius, about A.D. 51, of which Suetonius speaks

(*Claud.* 25; cf. Acts, XVIII, 2: "Because that Claudius had commanded all Jews to depart from Rome"). It was during these years, or possibly earlier, that Peter came to Rome, for it seems reasonably probable that he was there, nor would the whole matter be so violently disputed, were it not for a mistaken idea that its disproval would seriously discredit certain claims. In A.D. 61, Paul came to Rome and lived there for two years in his own hired house, very probably in the neighborhood of the *castra peregrinorum* on the Cælian Hill.

Thus Christianity began in Rome, and it remains to be seen what treatment it received at the hands of the Roman Empire. In judging of this treatment we ought not to forget that the distinction between Jews and Christians was of very gradual growth inside the church itself. How much more difficult would it, then, be for those outside to distinguish? The most characteristic mark of Judaism, its uncompromising monotheism, was common to both Jews and Christians. This was the bone of contention between the Empire and the Jews, and hence Roman officials instinctively classed them all together. It was only gradually that they realized the distinguishing mark between Jews and Christians, that the latter had a personal relation to the Founder of their religion. Neither Nero nor Domitian was, strictly speaking, a persecutor of Christians. The distinction was not as yet clear. It is only under Trajan that a real distinction begins to be made, and with the

rise of this distinction the persecution of the Jews practically stopped, for it was found that the aggressive
element was really the Christians. The Romans had
grown accustomed to the Jews; and though, theoretically, their monotheism was incompatible with the
state religion, the Roman Government had grown used
to it, and had learned that there was really no profit in
persecuting the Jews. But with these Christians it was
a different matter; and then, in very many cases, as
the Romans soon discovered, they were not Jews at
all by race. It might be well enough to connive at a
Jew's monotheism, but in the case of people who were
not Jews the matter was different. This new religion
was indeed a *religio illicita*, and it must be opposed.
Thus begins the long roll of Roman Emperors, who, as
a general rule in direct ratio to their strength and moral
qualities, became the persecutors of the Christians.
The best instance of a good emperor who tried to do
his duty conscientiously is shown us in the case of the
Emperor Trajan, in his correspondence with Pliny. This
correspondence is so instructive that I quote a few passages from it. Pliny writes to the emperor as follows
(*Ep.* 93 K.) :—

I am accustomed, Sire, to bring to thee all matters in which
I am in doubt. For who could better guide my uncertainty
or dispel my ignorance? I have never been involved in the
investigation of Christians. Therefore I do not know with
what measures or to what degree investigations should be carried on or penalties applied. I have hesitated much whether

youth deserves consideration, or whether there should be no
distinction between the weak and the strong, and whether
repentance should bring pardon, or whether repentance
should be of no avail if one had once been a Christian, or
whether a man should be punished for being a Christian, even
if he has committed no crimes, or whether we are punishing
the crimes that are connected with the belief. This is the
rule which I have followed in the case of those who have been
brought to my judgment seat, charged with being Christians.
I have asked them whether they were Christians, and when
they have confessed it, I have repeated my question a second
and a third time, and have threatened them with punishment. And when they have persisted, I have ordered them
to be punished. For whatever it might be that they were
guilty of, I did not doubt for a moment that their stub-
bornness and their inflexible obstinacy ought to be punished.
There are others affected by the same madness, whom I am
reserving to send to Rome because they are Roman citizens.
Soon after this, the accusations increased in number, as is
customary by force of publicity, and became of very many
different kinds. An anonymous list was published containing
a very large number of names. But these persons denied that
they are Christians or that they ever were, and in my presence
made sacrifice with incense and wine to the gods and also
to thy image, which I had caused to be brought in together
with the images of the gods. Moreover, they cursed Christ,
which they say that those who are truly Christians can never
be compelled to do. So I thought they ought to be acquitted.
And others who had been denounced to me confessed at first
that they were Christians and then denied it, saying that they
had been but had ceased to be, some of them several years
ago, and some even twenty years ago. All these worshiped
thy image and the images of the gods and cursed Christ.
Moreover, they asserted that this was the extent of their
fault or their mistake, that they were wont to meet together
on an appointed day before sunrise and sing hymns to the

praise of Christ as though in honor of a god, and that they
bound themselves by an oath — not for the purpose of crime,
but that they should not commit theft, robbery, or adultery,
that they should not break their promise or deny an obliga-
tion. And when they had done these things, they were wont
to depart and to meet again to partake in common of a harmless meal. And they added that after my edict, in which I,
according to thy orders, had forbidden these associations,
they had given up these customs. To discover the truth, I
deemed it necessary to put to the torture two female slaves,
who were said to have been initiated, but I discovered nothing
except an extraordinary and perverted superstition. And so
I have postponed the investigation and have come to you for
advice. For the matter seems to me to require consideration,
especially on account of the multitude of those involved in
danger. For large numbers of all ages and of all social conditions and of both sexes are involved and will be involved. For
the contagion of the evil has spread not only through the cities,
but through the villages and the farms. I think, however,
that it can be stopped and cured. Certain it is, that the
temples, which were so long deserted, are being frequented
again, and that the sacrifices, which were so long neglected,
are beginning to be performed again; and fodder for the sacrificial animals is beginning to be sold again, for which so long
it was difficult to find a purchaser. From this it is easy to
see how many men can be cured of the errors of their ways,
if only they be given a chance to repent.

Trajan's reply (*Ep*. 97) is equally characteristic: —

You have done what you ought to have done, my dear
Pliny, in investigating the cases of those who were brought
to you as Christians. In general it is impossible to lay down
any fixed principles in matters of this sort. One should not
proceed against them of one's own accord; if they are accused
and proved guilty, they must be punished. If, however, there
be any one who says he is not a Christian, and proves his as-

sertion by act, — that is, by sacrificing to our Gods, — even if he has been suspected in the past, he should be forgiven if he repents. Finally, in any sort of accusation an anonymous charge must not be considered, for that would set a very bad example and is contrary to the spirit of our time.

To be a Christian was in itself a crime against the state, because Christianity was a prohibited religion. It was a confusion of this statement which gave rise to the prevalent conception that the state persecuted Christians because they committed crimes. The one crime for which they were persecuted was the simple crime of being a Christian. There was another aspect of the case, however, by which the monotheism of the Christians, which prevented them from sacrificing to the gods of the Roman state, especially to the deified emperors, was in itself a crime against Roman religion.

But in general in the second century the law was allowed to lapse. This was the attitude of Hadrian and Marcus Aurelius. The psychological result of this laxness was that the Christians became constantly more bold in their opposition, and as martyrdom became more of a rarity, its allurements grew greater.

In these peaceful years of the latter half of the second century, especially in the reign of Marcus Aurelius, we have the interesting spectacle of "Plaintiffs" and "Defenders" discussing the merits of Christianity. There is Celsus, a Platonic philosopher, who wrote during the closing years of the reign of Marcus Aurelius. He is to be distinguished from Celsus, the Epicurean philosopher, who was a friend of Lucian. Origen and many others, following him, have confused the two. Celsus's book is called *The True Discourse*. It is an attempt to show Christians the folly and the evil of their attitude and to urge upon them the desirability of sacrificing such minor matters as personal belief to the patriotic instinct, which would make them support the religion of the state. It is not necessary that they should believe in the Roman gods, but it is their duty as gentlemen to support them for the good of the Roman state. It is not to be expected that such a cultured old-world philosophy would appeal to those who were living in the extraordinary state of problemless joy which seems to have surrounded the Christians of the first two centuries. And as a matter of fact, the book seems to have had no particular effect. Seventy years later, Origen ran across it and wrote a discourse disproving it. For us Celsus's book is lost, and we know its contents only through Origen; but fortunately the refutation is so conscientious and thorough, that it has been estimated that scarcely a tenth of Celsus's book is lost, and that we have at least three-quarters of it in direct quotation.

Much more interesting is the *Defence* or *Apologia* of Justin the Martyr. Justin, a native of Samaria, was a philosopher, one of that band of wanderers who called the whole world their country, and traveled from place to place, debating, lecturing, and writing. In his own intellectual wanderings he passed through various systems of philosophy, tarried for a while in Neoplatonism, but found no rest until he had adopted Christianity. But he saw no reason to change his outward mode of life, and continued to wear his philosopher's cloak. Thus he was able to speak to the masses with the freedom which the profession of philosophy always gives. His interest was naturally along the line of doctrine, and he was especially fond of attacking the heresies, which had already grown up within the church itself. His *Apologia*, which has been preserved to us, is a document more precious for its humanity than for its intellectual value. It explains the persecutions and the difficulties of the Christians as the work of demons, the facile explanation which remained in popularity for many centuries.

Thus, by the steady increase in numbers and by these open discussions, the Christian communities gradually rose into prominence, so that by the beginning of the third century they were a perfectly well-known element of the population. It is a great mistake to suppose that at this time they were secret organizations, concealing themselves, for example, under the guise of burial societies. To be sure, it is difficult to see what legal form their associations could take, for Christianity continued to be a prohibited religion. It is simply another case of tolerance, and it is a fact that during the whole of the third century their headquarters and the residences of their officials were perfectly well known to the state. If they were not persecuted, it was because they were officially tolerated, and if they were persecuted, the state had no difficulty in arresting immediately all their leaders. The actual church property itself, their places of assembly, and especially their burial-places, the Catacombs, could of course be held in the names of individuals.

In our respect for the majesty of Roman law and for the perfection of imperial organization, we must not forget that there were limits even to these great powers. Persecution had become a very serious matter; unless it were undertaken with a willingness to exert a very great pressure, it was apt to end in a farce. For example, when a certain proconsul of Asia began to persecute the Christians in a certain town, and the entire population, eager for martyrdom, crowded to his tribunal, having neither the strength nor the desire to obliterate the whole town, he could only turn on them in wrath and ask, in case they were so anxious to die, were there not ropes enough to hang themselves with, and cliffs enough from which they might leap to destruction — an attempt at humor which was so misplaced as only to emphasize his own embarrassment. Under the rule of the Severi (A.D. 193–235), it is only the first, Septimius Severus, who shows any hostility towards the Christians, and even then his son, Caracalla, was being brought up by a Christian nurse. We hear of the promulgation of an edict forbidding concessions to Judaism and Chris-

tianity, but we do not hear much of its results. The last
of the Severi, Alexander, a man of very catholic religious
disposition, included the Christians in the embrace of
his tolerance, grouped Christ with Orpheus, Abraham,
and Cicero in his chapels of hero-worship, and even contemplated raising a temple to the Founder of Christianity
and to include him officially among the gods of the state.
Fortunately this plan was never carried out.

A reaction was inevitable, and it came in the person
of the Emperor Decius (A.D. 250). It was patriotism,
and hatred of the Christians because they were unpatriotic, which moved Decius to his persecutions. He was
grieved at the constant increase of those who did not
worship the gods of the Roman state. So long as a man
sacrificed to the gods of the state, he might hold in private
any religion that he pleased. But a religion which forbade these national sacrifices must be suppressed. So
purely formal was his requirement that it might be a
perfunctory sacrifice only once offered, and those who
yielded thus gracefully would be rewarded with a certifi-
cate or diploma, which would free them from further
trouble and annoyance. Surely the Christian apologists
might well think that the demons themselves had invented such a tempting proposition. It had its natural
effect. On all sides men sought for these certificates.

Whole communities thus made their peace, notably at
Alexandria; and so weak had the passion for martyrdom
grown, that those who would not sacrifice went into

hiding to escape death. A few years ago some of these certificates of sacrifice were found in Egypt. They are pathetic documents bearing witness to the weakness of human nature, yet in some ways our respect for these men is as great as for those who at other times in a frenzy of devotion unnecessarily courted death.

And so we arrive at the last persecution, that by Diocletian. It took the Emperor a considerable time to make up his mind to engage in this persecution, and even when it began, the area of it was restricted to that part of the Empire which was more immediately under his personal observation. But by degrees the contagion of activity spread, and the greatest of the persecutions reached its full extent and power. It was a campaign of destruction, and every effort was made to eradicate entirely the existence of Christianity. Churches were destroyed, the holy books were burned, and the property of the church was confiscated by the state. Those holding office in the church were put to death; Christian laymen of high rank were removed from any official position which they might hold, and forbidden to hold office in the future; Christians of the lower classes were reduced to slavery; and Christian slaves were made slaves for life. The persecution began February 23, 303; it ceased with Galerius's edict of toleration, April 30, 311.

This brings us into the time and presence of Constantine. Constantine was born, in 280, in Dacia, the son of Constantius Chlorus and Helena, a woman of low birth, the daughter of an innkeeper. In 306, when his father, Constantius Chlorus, died at York, Constantine was at his side and was immediately saluted by the troops as his successor. For the following seventeen years his life was one long series of vicissitudes and struggles, until in 323 he became autocrat of the whole Empire, reigning as sole emperor, with four subordinate prefects. These struggles are extremely interesting, but we have no time to follow them in detail.

Virgil has often been accused of the lack of character in his hero Æneas, who has been likened to the pen-point with which the gods wrote history. But the description is still more true of Constantine. He accomplished an extraordinary number of fateful things, yet we feel that these things did themselves through him rather than that he did them. His official recognition of Christianity and his removal of the capital to Constantinople were both of them the necessary preconditions of all subsequent Western history; and yet in neither of these events do we feel that he who did them was at all conscious of what he was doing. His relation to Christianity is one of the riddles of history; and even the church itself is divided about him, because the East made him a saint while the West failed to do so. The story of his conversion is very uncertain; and the vision of the cross in the sky, which appeared as he was marching into Italy, and which he placed as the *labarum* on the banner of his troops as they marched to fight Maxentius at Saxa Rubra, may well have been a confusion in his mind between Mithras and Christianity. Constantine seems to have been originally a worshiper of the Sun-God, and we have a curious passage in Julian's writings (*Or.* 7, p. 228 D), in which he tells how Constantine, abandoning the worship of the Sun, "brought misfortune upon himself and upon his house."

The truth is that he does not seem to have been a religious man. He was not so much irreligious as unreligious. Politics meant much more to him than religion, and the unique opportunity of binding all the Christians in the Empire to his throne, by making Christianity the state religion, appealed to him much more than the inherent merits of Christianity itself. But there may also have been another consideration, which would have been entirely characteristic of Constantine and of the age in which he lived. He seems to have been an extremely superstitious man, and he may well have recognized the fact that all the emperors before him who had persecuted the Christians, had come to a sad end, and that when he marched against Maxentius, the avowed protector of the gods of Rome, he had been most unexpectedly successful. It would thus have been in a spirit of destiny that he marked his banners with the name of Christ and marched forward to Saxa Rubra.

So far as his interest in Christianity is concerned, we may trace two distinct epochs in his life, a period from about 311 until 324, during the time when he was fighting against Maxentius and later against Licinius, and when his attitude toward Christianity is merely the justification of it as a legally permitted religion of the Roman state, thus putting it on a par with the other existing worships; and a second period, beginning in 324 and continuing until his death, in 337, when he takes a more personal interest in Christianity and uses his influence to exalt it above the other cults of Rome.

But when once Christianity had been established, it is entirely characteristic of him that he should have been determined to make a success of it and to carry it through. It was then that, like Henry the Eighth, he was angered at the lack of an exact definition of Christianity. He had undertaken to see this new religion established, and now there seemed to be a doubt as to exactly what this religion was. Hence the Council of Arles in 316, and of Nicæa in 325, and his own constant attendance and deep interest in the latter. It was a strange spectacle, this vision of the successor of the deified emperors, himself still Pontifex Maximus of the old state religion, presiding over the bishops who were composing that historic statement, the Nicæan Creed.

Thus we pass to his successor, Constantius (337–361), whose only interest in Christianity was in theological dispute. Ammianus (XXI, 16) gives us a vivid picture of the effects of such a patronage. I quote it in Gibbon's words, because his translation gives unconsciously the whole spirit of Ammianus: —

The Christian religion, which in itself is plain and simple, he confounded by the dotage of superstition. Instead of reconciling the parties by the weight of his authority, he cherished and propagated, by verbal disputes, the differences which his vain curiosity had excited. The highways were covered with troops of bishops, galloping from every side to the assemblies, which they call synods; and while they labored to reduce the whole sect to their particular opinions, the public establishment of the posts was almost ruined by their hasty and repeated journeys.

Christianity had won the day. In numbers and in power she had outrun the other religions of the Orient. She had conquered in the battle against the Roman State. We must ask ourselves why she had been able to accomplish these things. It is obvious that from the physical standpoint she had been handicapped in the struggle.

In the first place, the religion of the Roman State, with its strong appeal of patriotism, was not in opposition to any other Oriental cult, and yet we have seen how by degrees its whole forces were turned against Christianity. In the second place, the other Oriental religions established and preserved an informal relationship, so that friction between them is very rare. This fellowship on their part was largely increased by their banding together to fight Christianity. Thus in her rivalry she was pitted, not against one of them, but against them all. As for the last element in the religious community, the doctrines of philosophy, she was opposed by them also, to the extent that they tended to create heresies and thus to break up the unity of her body.

In the last analysis, however, we see in the third and fourth centuries three great contending forces: Neoplatonism, Mithraism, and Christianity. It was around them that the battle raged, the struggle of masses against masses, but even more important, the struggle of the individual soul. Each of these forces came in succession to the front and gained at least a temporary control of the Empire: Mithras in the person of Diocletian; Christianity in Constantine; and Neoplatonism in Julian.

The three doctrines had many points of resemblance. They were all of them interested in the soul of man; they all offered the possibility of purifying that soul from its guilt; and they all promised eternal life. But Mithras and Christianity had at least two great advantages over Neoplatonism, advantages which gave them a much wider appeal than was possible for her. These advantages were their definiteness and their organization. Both Mithraism and Christianity possessed a definite body of doctrine. Their followers were not lost in philosophical speculation. There were certain clearly defined things to be believed, and more important yet, there was an equally definite set of things to be done. They possessed the appeal of a definite activity. To be sure, it was faith by which the soul was saved, but it was a great consolation to have an occupation.

The other advantage of Mithraism and Christianity

over Neoplatonism was in the matter of organization. Religion was reinforced by the social instinct. Men need not abide alone, immersed in solitary thought. They were gathered together in communities. The church organization, which Mithraism and Christianity alone possessed among all the cults of the Orient, was in the long run a great source of strength to them, even though, in the case of Mithraism, it was probably the only reason why it was not admitted as an official state cult. It is not difficult, therefore, to see why Neoplatonism was left behind in the race.

But at first sight it seems difficult to distinguish between Mithraism and Christianity. In judging of Mithras we ought never to forget that what we know of it we learn almost exclusively from its adversaries. We are justified, therefore, in positing for it a very lofty ethical standard. Its requirements of its devotees were absolutely genuine, and they were of a very high order. It is easy to say that the sacred books of Christianity may have helped her, the wonderful Old Testament which our narrow-minded modern age has so disastrously neglected. It is indeed a marvelous thing to read there the development of a god-concept throughout centuries of human history. But Mithras, too, had his sacred literature. It, too, went back from Rome to Asia Minor, from Asia Minor to Persia, from Persia to India. It, too, could show a marvelous religious development.

We talk of the ethical teachings of Jesus, but to a large

extent these ethical maxims, excellent as they are, were current in the ancient world. They were not the exclusive property of Christianity, but of this more in a moment.

There are, however, two elements of distinction. Christianity had beyond doubt a great psychological advantage over Mithraism in the presence of a Founder, whose life for these early Christians had a reality and a vividness which we to-day can scarcely realize. The oral tradition of this life still existed, and men could still connect themselves with it by going back only a few generations in their ancestry. Allowing for the difference of standpoint, Mithras might compare with Jehovah in matter of venerability, but Mithras possessed no parallel to Jesus of Nazareth, not as the savior of the world, for that Mithras could claim to be, but as the man Jesus, the carpenter's son. Of course such parallels were attempted, not to be sure in the cult of Mithras, but in the realm of philosophy. To please the Empress Julia Domna, Philostratus wrote the life of Apollonius of Tyana, a Pythagorean philosopher and miracle-worker of the first century of our era. It has often been asserted that the purpose of Philostratus was to present Apollonius not merely as the type of the perfect man, but as an avowed parallel to Jesus. But this latter assertion does not seem correct. The life was written without reference to Jesus, but rather in the attempt to produce a picture of an ideal philosopher. Nevertheless comparisons between the two lives inevitably suggested themselves; and such a comparison is all that is necessary to answer the question as to their relative ethical beauty. This personal relation to the Founder has always been characteristic of certain forms of Christianity, and it has doubtless had a very considerable effect, but it is open to grave question as to whether this in itself is sufficient to account either for the early conquest of Christianity or for its subsequent spread.

Here, however, a totally different principle steps in. Christianity has existed, at least in name, for nineteen hundred years. All the world, including its followers, are only too ready to admit that its practice has been far inferior to its theory. The difference between practice and theory has often grown so great that many parts of the theory have been forgotten. There is, however, one ideal of Christianity which seems never to have been forgotten, though its practice has more often been confined to the humbler classes, with occasional brilliant exceptions in the upper ones. We can scarcely conceive of two characters more essentially different than that of Augustine and that of Friedrich Nietzsche, and yet these two men agree with each other and with the man in the street regarding the essential characteristic of Christianity. It was this characteristic which caused Augustine to accept it after passing through Mithraism and Neoplatonism. It was this same characteristic which caused Friedrich Nietzsche to reject it as the "Sclavenmoral," the ethic of slavery. It is what we, who have the privilege of living in these post-Darwinian days, may call its opposition, the resistance which it offers to the working of the doctrines of biological evolution, its war against the practice of the survival of the fittest. To lift up those who have fallen beneath the feet of the progress of the world, to care for those who are of no apparent profit or good to society at large, to give to those who cannot give again, these are the deeds which even in our modern parlance we call "real Christianity." This is the "Sclavenmoral"; it does indeed hinder human progress, if by human progress is meant the Superman who gains added height by treading on those who are weaker than he. We may take Nietzsche's part against Christianity, we may have steeled ourselves by dint of scientific and pseudo-humanitarian thought so that we advocate euthanasia and lethal chambers, but somewhere inside of us is the chord which responds to the Christian note. It is this note which has awakened a response in millions of human beings during these nineteen centuries. It is the essentially new thing which has come into the world during this new régime. Neoplatonism and Mithraism knew nothing of it; and to its presence, so far as our phenomenal explanations go, was owing the conquest of Christianity over the combined forces of the ancient world.

CHAPTER V

JULIAN CALLED THE APOSTATE: THE TWILIGHT OF
THE GODS

IT is unquestionably true that to a very large extent the fourth century is a century of destruction, and no normally constituted man takes pleasure in destruction. A work of destruction may indeed be carried on on such a large scale that it inspires the beholder by the majesty of its action. But in this case it is the exhibition of power, rather than the destruction itself, which calls forth our reverence. But there is little of this in the fourth century. It is a period of steady almost monotonous annihilation of the outward features of paganism. It is much more than that. It is the dissolution of the old world in all its phases.

The question has often been asked, Was Christianity responsible? At first sight it seems as though this were the case. It is notorious that the Christians took very little interest in the affairs of the state. The reason for this indifference is not to be sought in any particular hostility on their part against Rome. But there was an Oriental element in early Christianity, an accentuation of the value of the life to come, and a corresponding indifference to the life that is. This detachment was particularly strong in the early history of the church.

But it was too purely an Oriental idea to be able to retain its strength in the Western world. It Has survived, but more in theory than in practice, and by a process of accommodation so that a real, even if secondary, value is assigned to the present life. But the willingness with which the early Christians accepted these Oriental ideas was itself dependent upon conditions for which Christianity was not responsible. The acceptance was a result rather than a cause, and the cause itself must be sought much farther back. It lay in the excessive cosmopolitanism of the Empire. It was this, rather than the doctrines of any particular religion, which had sapped the vitality of patriotism.

This is said in justice, and not in any spirit of excessive partiality toward the Christians of the fourth century. There are very few centuries in which Christianity makes a weaker appeal. The so-called early Christians are extremely interesting. If we study them sympathetically, we experience the contagion of their inspiration. We may not feel that their mental attitude is altogether healthy, but I venture to say that it was much more healthy in reality, and at the time, than it seems to us at this distance. But for the Christians of the fourth century there is very little to be said. Christianity had conquered. Her followers had obtained imperial patronage and political power. They were now experiencing the relaxing effects of success. They were becoming of the world, worldly. Men had received a beautiful

religion, and had shown their love of it by their willingness to die for it; but when they were asked to live for
it, they failed. They had defeated old Roman religion,
and it seemed to them that the battle was over. But their
greatest struggle was still before them. They were now
entering into the period of conflict between the old culture and the new religion. The world could afford to
lose the old religion, but it could not afford to lose the
old culture. Here victory lay not in destruction, but in
transformation and adoption. Success here was possible
only by humility, and they were soon to learn a lesson
of humility.

Thus, if we take the deeper view, we shall see that
this century is not one of mere destruction. The processes of accommodation are at work, and very much
that was good in pagan culture was ultimately to be
preserved. Then, too, if the Christians are in the main
not pleasing to behold, the last of the pagans are by
contrast extremely attractive. They have, to be sure, the
charm of the lost cause, and they are beautiful in their
death. But the beauty is genuine, and our admiration
is justified.

Let us consider for a moment the condition of that
old religion of the Roman State, that venerable system
of gods, priesthoods, and cult practices, whose origin
is lost in the darkness of early Roman history. For as
yet paganism was not officially abolished. Constantine
had elevated Christianity into a legitimate religion: he

had made it a state religion and had shown it his own personal favor; but paganism still abounded; it was still powerful enough to consider a renewal of the battle. In the struggle with Christianity it was confronted by a religion which possessed two things which it did not possess: an established dogma and a definite system of organization. Paganism, and above all Roman paganism, had never been dogmatic. It had concerned itself very little with the theory and the nature of the gods; it had confined itself almost exclusively to the methods by which the gods could be put to practical use. It found itself, therefore, in the fourth century, in the possession of no dogma; and in an age whose chief recreation was theological and philosophical dispute this was a very serious lack. Then, too, the old religion had always been synonymous with the state. Apart from the state it had had no organization. There had been no need of any such organization. Its place was assured to it. It had neither need nor desire to make converts. But now all this was changed. It still received the support of the state, but it had become involved in a competition, for which it was in no wise prepared. Its priesthoods were filled with men of affairs, who had neither time nor inclination to devote themselves to religious things, and it had no appeal except the appeal of patriotism; and now that the emperors acknowledged Christianity, its followers could no longer be openly accused of being unpatriotic. Thus its patriotic appeal was reduced to a mere sentimentalism. Christianity might now be the religion of the fatherland, but it was certainly not the religion of the fathers. But that was the extent of the argument.

The division of power between Christianity and paganism was not the same in all parts of the Empire. Christianity had begun in the Eastern provinces. It was but natural that its strength should be greatest there. Then, too, the capital was now in the East, and where the court was, there the newer things, among them Christianity, would naturally thrive. Ever since Caracalla had granted universal citizenship, and more especially since Constantine had founded Constantinople, Rome had become steadily more and more provincial. She had fallen behind in the advance of progress. She had grown distinctly old-fashioned. But among these old fashions was paganism, so that the city of Rome itself was the greatest stronghold of paganism in the whole Empire. There was also another reason why paganism flourished at Rome. The Senate had never ceased to exist. It had not been transferred to Constantinople, but instead a new Senate had been created there, while the old Senate continued in Rome. The Senators of Rome were conservative, and being conservative they were for the most part pagan. Thus Rome was in a sense an exception to the general lack of pagan organization. She was provided with such an organization in the shape of the Senate. At the end of the fourth century there were still in existence in Rome over four hundred pagan temples. The Magna Mater was still worshiped, and sacrifices were still made at the Ara Maxima, the old altar of Hercules in the Forum Boarium. In 359, the Prefect of Rome, in accordance with ancient custom, sacrificed to Castor and Pollux at Ostia. Inscriptions to Mithras are still very numerous, and a *taurobolium* was performed near Saint Peter's as late as 390. But these are exceptional conditions, and throughout the Empire at large Christianity was making steady progress.

And yet it might readily seem that the instincts of paganism would perhaps respond to a strong and earnest appeal. Thus we are introduced to Julian, called the Apostate. We shall take occasion later to form an opinion of Julian's character and his significance; but it may be as well to say, at the start, that the judgments passed on his character may be divided into two classes: those which belittle his significance and have usually emanated from the supporters of Christianity, and those which exaggerate his importance and have been held by the opposers of Christianity, notably by the immortal Gibbon. And yet it is Gibbon's wonderful account of Julian which lies at the back of all our modern feeling toward him. This is true of every one of us, whether we have read Gibbon's account or not, for Gibbon's description has entered so permeatingly into the web and woof of all that has been written about Julian, that Gibbon is, directly or indirectly, the source of almost all

that we have ever heard of Julian. We may well consider Gibbon's point of view as prejudiced. We may be
able to analyze that prejudice and strive thus to avoid it,
but we shall strive in vain to escape the influence of
Gibbon. Nor is it to be desired that we should altogether
escape it, for in so doing we should lose a certain amount
of legitimate charm. We shall find that Julian was not
a supremely great man, but we shall find him genuine
and sincere and very lovable, at least to those who
understand him. It is a great pleasure to have the privilege of discussing him.

Julian was born in 331; he died in 363; he lived therefore only thirty-two years. For the understanding of
what he did, we must remember his youthfulness. His
early education is indicative of the dualism which then
existed between the old pagan culture and the new
Christian faith. He had two tutors, the excellent but
uninspiring Eusebius of Nicomedia, Bishop of Constantinople, who taught him the Bible; and the sympathetic Mardonius, a eunuch who had been tutor to
Julian's mother, and who now opened to him the beauty
of Homer. In 337, Constantine died, and Constantius
organized a general massacre of all his relatives. Only
two were saved. They were the six-year-old Julian and
his older brother Gallus, who was then eleven. Seven
years of comparative peace followed, but when Gallus
was eighteen and Julian thirteen (344), the Emperor
Constantius deemed it wise to keep them both in close

observation, and they were confined for six years in a fortress near Cæsarea in Cappadocia. Their prison was, to be sure, an ancient palace, where once the kings of Cappadocia had resided. Its grounds were extensive and the two princes were surrounded by everything which might make life happy except freedom itself, without which all the rest was of no profit.

Finally, in 351, the elder brother, Gallus, was declared Cæsar and married to the Princess Constantina. Gallus at Cæsarea had been sufficiently a sad spectacle, but Gallus as an emperor was infinitely worse. His violent temper brought him into difficulty with all those about him, and his wife, instead of being a help, was a constant incentive to evil. Thus he aroused the hatred of Constantius, and was finally put to death at Pola in 354. In the same year Julian, who was then living in Ionia, was taken prisoner and carried to Milan. There for seven months he was kept a prisoner with the constant menace of death. Owing to the good offices of the Empress Eusebia, gradually a more favorable view of his case was taken, and he was permitted to go into exile at Athens. But though it might be nominally exile, it was for a Julian a veritable coming into his own. These were the years in which his tendencies to mysticism were beginning to develop. While not unmindful of the fact that the preservation of his life was owing to the Empress Eusebia, he felt nevertheless that it was the gods of Greece who had used her as their human instrument.

And now he was permitted to go to the heart of that Greek world which he loved so dearly. He was to study in that place, which was not only historically the centre of Greek thought, but was in his day so full of learning and teaching that it was not unlike a modern university.

Julian's remembrances of these six months and his permanent affection for Athens are very beautifully expressed in Gibbon's phrase: "Julian inviolably preserved for Athens that tender regard which seldom fails to arise in a liberal mind from the recollection of the place where it has discovered and exercised its growing powers." Gregory of Nazianzus gives an account of Julian's appearance during these student days. He describes his nervousness and excitability, his stuttering and irregular speech, and strives to produce the impression without actually saying it in words, that Julian belonged in the category of the epileptic. But Gregory's antipathy is well known, and nothing is so easy as to brand a person with the mark of abnormality, especially when that person has led of necessity a more or less solitary life. That Julian at this time was of a pensive and emotional temperament there is little doubt. He may well have been given to brooding over the mysteries of life, and we know that the sense of his messiahship was beginning to dawn upon him, and that he felt himself the favorite of the gods, protected by a guard of angels. But the preservation of his mental balance is proved to us beyond a peradventure by his marvelous success in the activities of life upon which he was now called to enter.

Without the understanding of these first twenty-four years of his life, the last eight are a complete riddle. It is little wonder that he hated a religion which was presented to him theoretically in Hebrew, a language which he did not like, and worked out before him practically in the person of the murderous Constantius. It is not surprising that the imaginative little boy, with his love of Greek and the stories of Homer, should live more and more in that past heroic age rather than in a present which began for him in an atmosphere of murder, and continued in one of espionage and imprisonment. And the enforced companionship of a brutal and unsympathetic brother would serve only to accentuate his loneliness.

The happy student days in Athens came all too quickly to an end. The post of Cæsar in the West was vacant. The frontier was being threatened at several points, and Constantius had need of an assistant. It was again the Empress Eusebia who championed the cause of Julian, and succeeded in removing the Emperor's prejudices against him. Julian was recalled to Milan, married to Helena, Constantius's sister, appointed Cæsar November 6, 355, and sent to fight in Gaul and Germany against the enemies of Rome. It is little wonder that Julian was thoroughly terrified by this sudden change in his fortunes. When the long beard and the gray cloak of the philosopher were removed from him, and he was clad in the imperial purple, it was extremely natural that as he returned to the palace, he should murmur to himself the familiar line of the *Iliad* (v, 83), "Him purple death laid hold on and stern fate." The example of his brother Gallus was before him, for whom the purple had become the shroud. But however cast down he was at the moment, he made a brave showing before the soldiers, and immediately won their respect.

It is not difficult to see the ulterior purpose which Constantius may have had in this appointment. There were many chances that Julian would never return from Gaul or Germany. But Constantius reckoned without his host, and Julian's guard of angels stood him in good stead. Thus Julian was dispatched to Gaul; but the distrust of the Emperor surrounded him by a multitude of advisers and a large retinue of servants. Julian was restive under this tutelage, but judging the matter objectively, one can but admire the prudence of an emperor who hesitated to give uncontrolled command to a dreamy, absolutely inexperienced youth of twenty-four. It is the more to Julian's credit, however, that he succeeded under these trying circumstances in making his own individuality tell, and in giving such proof of his real ability that he was gradually allowed to assume control. Thus the philosopher became the soldier. The story that in the midst of military exercises he cried out, "O Plato! O Plato! What a task for a philosopher!"

may well be true, but it does not necessarily prove that the soldier's life was distasteful to him. On the contrary, it may well have been the expression of the throwing of himself wholesouledly into the task, buoyed up by the incongruity of the situation, which to his mystical mind would be only another proof of the activity of his guardian angels, and the working-out of the inevitable destiny by which he was to be given power in order that he might be the savior of his people.

But whatever doubt there may be concerning his enjoyment of the task, there is no doubt of his success in it. This has been admired even by his most energetic detractors, who, while still denying that he was a great general, are compelled to admit that he at least accomplished the work of a great general. He won the love and respect of his soldiers by the simple and time-honored method, which has never yet failed, and never can fail so long as human nature lasts, — that of sharing their hardships and privations. His first campaign (356) was concerned with the defense of Autun against the Alemanni, and of Cologne against the Franks. The winter of 356–57 was a very difficult one, for the Germans seemed ever present in Alsace, and were bold enough to besiege Julian himself at Sens. But Julian's revenge came quickly. In August, 357, with a slender army of thirteen thousand men he engaged in conflict at Strassburg with almost three times that number of barbarians. Largely owing to Julian's own courage, the Romans won a great victory. Of his subsequent campaigns in Gaul, of his three expeditions beyond the Rhine, and of his diligent restoration of the cities of Gaul, we have no time to speak.

He had succeeded, and the inevitable result of success followed, the jealousy of the Emperor. Constantius might console himself by sending letters to the provinces, omitting all mention of Julian's name, and talking of his own success against the barbarians, but all mankind, and Julian's troops above all, knew that when the battle occurred, the Emperor was at a safe distance of forty days' journey. Thus Constantius adopted another scheme, which bade fair to be more effective. Gaul was in comparative peace, while the Eastern provinces were in a state of turmoil. Circumstances, therefore, offered to Constantius a plausible excuse for transferring to the East four of the legions under Julian, in their entirety, and picked men from the others. Julian had no choice but to obey, and accordingly bade farewell to his faithful troops, making them a final speech on a plain near Paris. They heard him in silence, but that same day at midnight they surrounded the palace, which was on the Rive Gauche, in the modern Rue de la Harpe, and proclaimed Julian Emperor. All night long he defended himself against them, but at dawn they broke in and carried him away, to be publicly saluted by the army. He refused to be crowned by a woman's necklace or a horse collar, but accepted a soldier's neck-chain as the symbol of the crown.

Then followed a year of anxious waiting, filled with fruitless negotiations between the two Emperors, Julian in Gaul, Constantius in Cappadocia, while each man stayed at his post, unable to leave without damage to the Empire, and each preferring his public duty to his private interest. Finally, in 361, Julian marched eastwards, to attack Constantius, and Constantius on his part moved westward to attack him. But long before the armies met, while Julian was still on the Danube, Constantius died near Tarsus, November 3, 361, and his troops surrendered to Julian, who was thus acclaimed by the whole Empire.

It was December 11, 361, when Julian entered Constantinople; it was June 26, 363, that he was killed by the Persian dart. There remained for him, therefore, eighteen and one half months of life, in which to carry out the real purpose for which the six long years of soldiering had been only the preparation; yet even of these precious months, three — the last three — were destined to be consecrated to the Persian campaign in which he lost his life. For his religious reforms there were left, therefore, only a little over fifteen months.

The idea at the base of all of Julian's activity was the establishment of the "Holy Church of Paganism." His belief in the pagan gods and his conservative instincts convinced him that a return to the religion of the fathers was essential for the salvation of Rome. Yet his training in the Christian religion had been so thorough, and his knowledge of the world about him was so broad, that he realized that this renaissance of pagan belief would be possible only by the imitation and adaptation of those new elements which Christianity and certain of the Oriental religions had brought into existence. Both Christianity and Mithraism had two great advantages over the later state religion of paganism. They were in possession of a system of dogma and of a definite organization. It was these advantages which he hoped to gain for the followers of the old religion.

But here the pathos of the situation came in. There is no doubt that Julian thought of himself as a genuine Roman, there is no doubt that he supposed he was establishing old Roman religion. But he was much more Greek than Roman, and the religious ideas which he attempted to establish belonged not in the realm of Roman thought, but rather in that of Neoplatonism. It was the Church of Hellenism in which he was interested. In the matter of dogma his difficulties were greatest. Neoplatonism was not only a philosophical system, but a peculiarly vague and mystical philosophy. It was the mystical element which caused it to appeal to Julian; but what appealed to Julian could not, in the nature of things, appeal to the masses. Neoplatonism was not for the common people; and be Julian's preparation of it never so careful, it could not but fail to be understood.

In the matter of organization he was more successful. It was a relatively easy matter for an emperor to reform the priesthoods. But he was not content with a mere improvement of outward form. It was not simply a question of keeping the priesthoods filled with respectable persons: the problem which Augustus had had to solve. The requirements of the priesthood had increased enormously since that day. Christianity and the other religions of the Orient had introduced into Rome the idea that the priestly office demanded constant and devoted service, and that its incumbents must possess a high degree of morality rather than mere worldly position. Thus Julian's reform of the pagan priesthood was distinctly a moral crusade and his letters on this subject resemble episcopal admonitions. The persons fitted to be priests are not those who are distinguished by wealth or birth, but rather those who are known for their love of the gods and men. They shall be held accountable for their actions. If they do wrong, they shall be punished. But so long as they hold their position, they deserve the respect of all men. They shall take their turn at the offering of sacrifice, and for the required number of days they shall give their undivided energy to the sacred tasks. They shall be of spotless purity both in mind and body. They shall be not merely ceremonially pure; they shall practice chastity and real holiness. Their lives shall be better than the lives of those about them, not only when they are officiating, but when they are living with their fellow men. They shall not frequent theatres or wineshops; they shall visit the Forum or the Palace

only on errands of justice or mercy. They shall not
read novels or comedies or satires, but instead history
and philosophy. They shall be chary even of their philosophers, avoiding the impiety of the Epicureans and the
Skeptics, and clinging to Pythagoras, Plato, and the
Stoics, such philosophy as teaches the existence of the
gods and the government of Providence.

Then, too, the services of the pagan church must be
made attractive. In imitation of the Christians, there
must be music and choir-boys. But Julian recognized
still another source of the strength of Christianity, its
practical benevolence, and to this he calls attention. It
is the indifference of the pagan priests toward the poor
which has suggested to these impious Galileans the idea
of practicing benevolence, and they have strengthened
their wretched propaganda by covering it with this virtuous exterior. They practice humanity toward strangers; they are at pains to give honorable burial to the
dead; and they lead virtuous lives. The pagan priesthood
should imitate them, and concern itself with the poor
and the unfortunate. He remarks that the Jews have no
beggars, and that the impious Galileans support not only
their own people but pagans as well. It is disgraceful
that the pagan poor should be deprived of the aid that is
owing them.

As for Julian himself, the feelings of his own messiahship seem to have grown upon him. The guard of angels
becomes more specific. He is a vessel chosen of the gods,

and his trust is in them. With his accession to the emperorship his allegiance to these gods had grown more outspoken; and just as Constantine had marched against Maxentius with the cross of Christ on his banners, so in the name of Jupiter Julian marched against Constantius. But it is unjust to think of Julian as a merely fanciful and distorted mind bent upon the restoration of a crass anthropomorphic polytheism. His is in great part a very beautiful and spiritual mysticism. He felt his loneliness, as all mystics do, and in his case the loneliness was increased by the inevitable solitude which surrounded the imperial throne. His trust in the gods is more than the resignation of the fatalist: it is touched with a loving confidence which is worthy of the highest Christianity; and this confidence is all the more remarkable because it seems to result from the overcoming of the feeling that God has become known to man for the first time in Christianity. He seems inclined to believe this, and yet he conquers this inclination and asserts the historical doctrine of a continuous revelation. "It is wrong to praise the men of old without following their ensample, and to suppose that while God was eager to help them, he will neglect those who to-day practice virtue, for the sake of which God found pleasure in them," and again, in a moment of depression, "God will perhaps provide something good, for it is not probable that he who has intrusted himself to the gods will be neglected or left alone."

His own suspicions that he may fail in his task are splendid proofs of sanity, for the genuine paranoiac has few such doubts; and surely we should hesitate to characterize his reliance on the gods as insanity simply because he called his deity by a different name. Had he succeeded instead of failing, we should look upon him as one of the greatest figures in religious history. For his work was inevitably doomed to failure. Roman religion was dead, and even had it not been dead, it could not have been quickened into newness of life by the reinforcement of Neoplatonism.

It was not by his positive and constructive work, but by his negative and destructive work, that he produced a lasting effect. It is little wonder that Julian's hostility to Christianity aroused great uneasiness among the Christians. Men were still alive who remembered the severity of Diocletian's persecutions. Then, too, there was an added horror in Julian's case, because of his intimate acquaintance with Christianity and its sacred books. It was sufficiently disagreeable to be fined, without suffering the additional taunt of "how hardly shall a rich man enter into the kingdom of Heaven." There was also a peculiar aggravation in his attitude toward the Jews. His fondness for the Jews has usually been attributed to his desire to irritate the Christians, but this is unjust. His fondness for them was genuine. It was founded partly on his own mysticism, which found response in their worship of the mysterious Jehovah, and it was quickened by the Jewish elements in his beloved Neoplatonism.

But all these are small things compared to the one great work, which in the history of culture Julian was called upon to do. This was the famous edict against the Christian teachers of rhetoric, which was promulgated just twelve months before his death. Here again he has been accused of malice, and yet the facts of the case are far otherwise. For us to-day the immortal gods of Homer and Virgil are merely the paraphernalia of mythology, a beautiful poetic symbolism. But for the pagans of Julian's day they were living realities. We need no better proof of this than the fact that these gods were so real to the Christians, too, that they thought of them as demons. There was, therefore, legitimate ground for offense at the thought of Christian teachers expounding Homer and Virgil to their Christian pupils, and being careful to destroy all reverence for Jupiter and Minerva and Apollo. It was quite improper that Christians should desire to learn such things, and if they did, they should go to the pagan masters, who could teach them properly. Otherwise let them be content with their own religious literature, their "Matthew and Luke," which they could interpret according to their own sweet will.

This edict was the most brilliant stroke of Julian's policy, and it had the most far-reaching results. From Julian's standpoint the carrying-out of this edict would deal the deathblow to Christianity. Christians would not permit their children to attend these schools kept by pagan teachers; and yet these were the only schools in which ancient literature was taught. Thus the rising generation would inevitably have been divorced from culture, and thus the Christian Church would have sunk into a position of inferiority simply because of its ignorance. Its leaders would be affected in the same fashion, and the Christian clergy, instead of being experts in theology and philosophy, would be blind and leaders of the blind.

Thus the problem was fairly stated. Are ancient religion and ancient culture inseparable? Does the breakdown of ancient religion necessitate the destruction of ancient culture? Christians were thus brought face to face with their relation to the admirable heritage of pagan thought. The problem took centuries to solve. It was almost two hundred years before the first definite steps in this direction were taken.

Meantime, though the edict itself was soon repealed, the inconsistency in the matter was brought home to the minds of the Christians. They did not feel that their own holy books created a sufficient body of literature. They admitted the holiness of these books, but it is very questionable whether they were fond of them. The Old Testament especially seems to have been thoroughly distasteful. Very probably the fact that they held it in common with the Jews made it seem less desirable. They must, however, have a literature, and if pagan literature were not proper for them, they must construct one of their own. Hence the curious imitation of the classics in the doggerel of the Christian poets, the attempts to make a Homer out of the Old Testament, a Plato out of the Gospels, to say nothing of Christian odes in the style of Pindar. The effects of this new attitude toward pagan literature soon became evident on all sides. It is not far from this time that Jerome — who loved Cicero's writings and his style far better than the Hebrew Scriptures, which he was to make into the Vulgate — finished a day of fasting by reading Cicero. Thereupon, as he tells us so graphically, "a high fever seized upon my wearied body and my limbs were racked with such terrible heat that it seemed as though they would fall apart. Already the preparations for my burial were being begun; and the warmth of life had left my body and I was cold, except that my breast was still warm and my heart beat fiercely. Suddenly I had the sensation as though I were being brought to the judgment seat. There, there was so much light, and such glory shone from those who stood about, that I fell upon my face and did not dare to raise my eyes. Then one asked me who I was and I answered, 'A Christian' (*Christianus sum*); 'No!' said the Judge, 'thou art not a Christian, thou art a Ciceronian; for where thy heart is, there is thy treasure also' (*non Christianus, Ciceronianus es*). Then I was silent, and felt the pain of the blows with which they chastised me." Yet Jerome's story is only one of a long list of such bat-

tles, fought out in individuals, between the instinct for
the old culture and the power of the new religion.

Thus Julian had his effect, and by this one deed alone
his life would be justified. But he was influential in other
and less tangible ways. When the Persian campaign put
an end to his life, there followed nineteen years of religious peace (363–82), a precious interlude in which many
treasures of art and architecture were saved. Yet these
nineteen years of peace were possible only because of
Julian's reign of nineteen months. Thus Julian passes
out of our story, and as he does so we may listen to his
dying words. They have been preserved for us by Ammianus, who heard them spoken, and though they may
well have been prepared in advance and made ready
against the event, there is an impressive dignity about
them, especially in Gibbon's admirable translation,
which I quote, and they afford us a clear insight into
that combined sense of duty toward men and trust in
God which was the keynote of Julian's life.

Friends and fellow soldiers, the seasonable period of my departure is now arrived, and I discharge, with the cheerfulness
of a ready debtor, the demands of Nature. I have learned
from philosophy how much the soul is more excellent than the
body; and that the separation of the nobler substance should
be the height of joy rather than of affliction. I have learned
from religion, that an early death has often been the reward of
piety; and I accept, as a favor of the gods, the mortal stroke
which secures me from the danger of disgracing a character,
which has hitherto been supported by virtue and fortitude,
I die without remorse, as I have lived without guilt. I am

pleased to reflect on the innocence of my private life; and I can affirm with confidence, that the supreme authority, that emanation of the divine power, has been preserved in my hands pure and immaculate. Detesting the corrupt and destructive maxims of despotism, I have considered the happiness of the people as the end of government. Submitting my actions to the laws of Providence, of justice, and of moderation, I have trusted the event to the care of Providence. Peace was the object of my councils, as long as peace was consistent with the public welfare; but, when the imperious voice of my country summoned me to arms, I exposed my person to the dangers of war, with the clear foreknowledge (which I had acquired by the art of divination) that I was destined to fall by the sword. I now offer my tribute of gratitude to the Eternal Being, who has not suffered me to perish by the cruelty of a tyrant, by the secret dagger of conspiracy, or by the slow tortures of lingering disease. He has given me, in the midst of an honorable career, a splendid and glorious departure from the world; and I hold it equally absurd and equally base to solicit or to decline the stroke of fate. . . . Thus much I have attempted to say, but my strength fails me, and I feel the approach of death. I shall cautiously refrain from any word that may tend to influence your suffrages in the election of an emperor. My choice might be imprudent, or injudicious; and if it should not be ratified by the consent of the army, it might be fatal to the person whom I should recommend. I shall only as a good citizen express my hopes that the Romans may be blessed with the government of a virtuous sovereign.

The nineteen years of peace which followed Julian's death, and which coincide roughly with the reign of the Emperor Gratian, were destined to be brought to an end by this same Gratian, but under the influence of a great personality to whom we now turn. This is Ambrose, Bishop of Milan. He was born, probably at Trier, about

340, when Julian was nine years old. His father, who was Prætorian Prefect of the Gauls, died when Ambrose was twelve years old, and the boy went with his mother to Rome, where he received an excellent education. He was brought up in the Christian faith, and gave his especial attention to the study of law. Here he was so successful that at the age of thirty-two (372) he was appointed Governor of Liguria and Æmilia, and took up his official residence at Milan. In the third year of his governorship (374), Dionysius, the Catholic Bishop of Milan, and his rival, Auxentius, the Arian Bishop, both died, and a stormy election of a successor took place. In his capacity of Governor, Ambrose presided at the election. Then the extraordinary thing happened, that both parties united in electing him to the bishopric. The anomaly of the situation did not fail to impress itself on those who were present, and the story arose, and it may well represent the truth, that when Ambrose was addressing the people in the church, urging upon them the necessity of maintaining order, suddenly above the sound of his own words arose the penetrating staccato note of a child's voice, saying with unconscious calm, "Ambrose is Bishop! Ambrose is Bishop." The child, who knew Ambrose by sight, seeing him standing in the place where the bishop was wont to stand, naturally concluded that he must therefore be bishop. His innocent words were a prophecy, and a few months later, after being baptized, Ambrose was consecrated. From that day

(December 7, 374) until Good Friday (April 4, 397), when he died, he was the most conspicuous figure in the Western world; about him are grouped the other characters, and he stands in some relation to every important event.

Whether or not we rejoice in him as a great prince of the church, and the predecessor of Gregory the Great in the work of establishing the temporal power, we must give him his fair due as one of the great characters of history, and we may be sure that had we known him we, too, should have loved him, as Augustine and so many others did. Every inch a man, fearless, straightforward, frank, open, and incessantly active, the world owes him a great debt; and it is only just to say that those elements in his character, of which we find it hard to approve, are the stamp of his age, and without them his popularity and therefore his power would not have been so great. There is no better way to study the history of the last third of this fourth century (363–95), than to follow the events in the life of Ambrose.

The first event, and one which was to have great consequences, was his friendship with the Emperor Gratian, who spent a large part of the three years 378–81 at Milan. Gratian was nineteen at the beginning of their intimacy, but he had been emperor for eleven years. He was destined to live only a few years longer, but during these years he was under the control of Ambrose, whom he called *parens*. It was Gratian who put an end to Julian's legacy of nineteen years of peace, by issuing in 382 a decree which amounted practically to the disestablishment of the pagan cults, the cutting of them off from the financial support of the state. Up to this time the nominally Christian emperors of Rome had done nothing to alter the financial relations between the Roman state and the old Roman religion. They had, indeed, changed the official relationship in almost no respect, and each had continued to be Pontifex Maximus. At an earlier period in his life, Gratian had rebelled against the inconsistency of this position, and when he had been offered the customary title of Pontifex Maximus and the white robe with the purple border, which the chief priest had been wont to wear, he had refused them both.

Now, doubtless at the instigation of Ambrose, he went still farther. The money of the state should no longer be spent for the support of pagan ceremonial and pagan priesthoods. The lands which the pagan cults possessed were confiscated; the money which had been used for the games went into the public treasure; and the money for the salaries of the Vestal Virgins was used to improve the postal service.

Then followed the same course of events as is usual in cases of disestablishment. At the moment of the shock private benefaction stepped in to fill the breach, and for the time being the resources of paganism were actually larger than they had been under the régime of the state. But this was only a momentary enthusiasm, and this newly acquired income soon ceased, either by the death of the benefactors or by the lessening of their zeal. So far as the public cults of paganism were concerned, they were doomed entirely aside from any legal prohibition.

It is Ambrose, again, who is the central figure in a very interesting controversy which arose at this time. It is the dispute over the removal of the altar of Victory from the Senate House (*Curia*). The new Senate House, which Julius Cæsar had begun in the corner of the Forum, was completed by Augustus, who, among other things, ornamented the altar of the Goddess Victoria, with a statue of the goddess, which had come from Tarentum, in southern Italy. The custom of offering a few grains of incense to Victoria had become a tradition in the Senate, and had gradually acquired the colorlessness of a stereotyped form. In addition, the abstract character of Victoria made her of no particular offense to the Christians. But certain more zealous members of the new religion finally prevailed upon Constantius to have it removed. Under Julian's régime it was naturally restored again, and now under Gratian it had been again removed. In itself it was a matter of no great significance, but it serves as an illustration not only of the pagan majority in the Senate, but also of the admirable character of some of these pagans, notably Quintus Aurelius Symmachus. In the course of ten years (382–91) four times an effort was made to have Victoria restored to her place. The first deputation journeyed north in vain, and never succeeded in having audience of the Emperor, for Pope Damasus sent a counter-petition, and this, with the influence of Ambrose, was sufficient to prevent the embassy from gaining a hearing. Two years later (384), nothing daunted, the pagan party again presented a petition, this time to Valentinian II, for Gratian was dead. The writer is Symmachus in his capacity of Prefect of the city of Rome. The arguments are stereotyped, but the eloquence is very great. Rome attained fame and glory under the old gods. With the coming of this new religion her power has been declining. To this new religion must be attributed the disasters which she has undergone, especially the famine of the past year. It is Roma herself who is speaking, and she pleads for tolerance and liberty in her old age.

Ambrose himself answered this petition. It is not the gods of the state who saved Rome. In fact, on occasions they actually failed, as when the Gauls captured the city, or when Hannibal approached the walls. It was not their religion, but their own energetic character which made the Romans what they were. We may not admire the argument, but it was successful, and again the petition was refused.

But the struggles of Ambrose were not confined to his contest with the Senate. There were more vital conflicts nearer at hand, notably with the empress-mother, Justina (the widow of Valentinian I, the mother of Valentinian II, and the mother-in-law of Theodosius). She was an Arian, and interested in the spread of this heresy, and anxious to obtain for it various churches in Milan. She requested that the Portian Basilica, which lay outside the city, should be given to the Arians. When this was refused, a request was made for the new basilica, in the city itself, and when this, too, was denied, she proceeded to take the Portian Basilica by force. But Ambrose and his followers held the church, and the matter ended without bloodshed, in the defeat of the Empress. A year later (January 23, 386), matters came again to a climax, when the young Valentinian, at the instance of the Empress, demanded that Ambrose should either yield to his request or leave the city. Then the figure of Ambrose stood forth in all its majesty. From the very beginning it has not been a mere discussion regarding heresy, a far greater principle has been at stake. It is the principle of the domination of the church. And now the time is ripe for the full expression. The church may indeed judge laymen, but laymen should not judge the church, and an emperor is after all only a layman. There is no question of Ambrose leaving the bishopric. Valentinian has nothing to say about it. It had been given to Ambrose by the unamimous vote of the people. As for Arianism, he will fight it to the death The rumor soon spread through the city, that Ambrose would be removed by force. He took up his residence in the basilica, where he was surrounded by his friends, who were willing and

eager to lose their lives in his defense. But the days of
waiting were wearisome, and even the ardor of those who
loved him best might well become cooled by inaction.
To give employment to the waiting people, he introduced
the antiphonal chant which has been forever named after
him. Thus he became the first great Latin hymn-writer
of the church, especially famous for the three wonderful
hymns: the hymn for Christmas, "Veni Redemptor
Gentium," the morning hymn, "Æterne Rerum Creator," and the evening hymn, "Deus Creator Omnium."
In the next chapter we shall meet with one of the audi-
tors of this new music, Augustine, into whose mind this
scene came back as he lay on his bed, crushed with grief
over the death of his mother. I quote the passage from
the *Confessions* in Bigg's translation: —

Then I slept and awoke and found my sorrow diminished
not a little. And as I lay alone upon my bed, I recalled the
truthful verses of thy servant Ambrose. For indeed thou
art

> Creator of the earth and sky,
> Ruling the firmament on high,
> Clothing the day with robes of light,
> Blessing with gracious sleep the night
> That rest may comfort weary men,
> And brace to useful toil again,
> And soothe awhile the harassed mind,
> And sorrow's weary load unbind.

There was nothing to be gained by fighting Ambrose.
Justina yielded; and the Arian heresy failed to receive
its church in Milan. Thus Ambrose had controlled

Gratian and had won his battle with Justina. But there remained for him the greatest conquest of all, that of Theodosius, a conquest all the more interesting because Theodosius was not an Arian, but Orthodox. In the year 390, the population of Thessalonica had incurred the wrath of Theodosius. In a moment of terrible anger he had ordered that the whole population should be put to death. On April 30, 390, the seventy-ninth anniversary of the day when Christianity had been made the religion of the Roman state, they were driven, or perhaps lured into the circus. The doors were shut, and for three hours the ghastly butchery continued. Between seven and fifteen thousand people were murdered.

When Ambrose heard of this terrible deed, he wrote to the Emperor, rebuking him for his action. But when Theodosius, instead of showing signs of repentance, actually presumed to enter the church at Milan, that church which is now worthily called S. Ambrogio, Ambrose met him at the door, and, if we may follow Theodoret, rebuked him, calling upon him to repent, and to realize the enormity of his act and the offense which he had committed against God, and bidding him depart to devote himself to penitence and prayer.

Theodosius obeyed, and after months of delay and useless attempts at reconciliation, Ambrose agreed that he should be pardoned, but only on two conditions: first, that he should do public penance, and second, that he should prepare a law requiring an interval of thirty days between the passing of a capital sentence and its execution.

On Christmas Day, 390, Theodosius entered the church and performed his penance. He bowed himself to the ground, smote his forehead, and repeated the twenty-fifth verse of the one hundred and nineteenth psalm: "My soul cleaveth unto the dust, quicken me according to Thy word." But even then his humbling was not complete; for when he went up the steps into the chancel to present his offering, as was the custom in the Eastern Church, Ambrose sent a deacon to tell him that his place was outside the chancel rail, that "purple makes emperors, not priests."

Scarcely could there be found a clearer proof than this that the ancient régime had passed, when an emperor, whose predecessors, less than a century before, had been themselves thought of as divine, and as proper objects of worship, humbles himself in the dust before the principles of a new religion, and at the command of one of its priests. As for the figure of the man who gave the command, the eye of the mind has no difficulty in looking forward from him to Gregory the Great, and from him to that other Gregory with Henry the Fourth at Canossa.

But there are many things yet to be done before we reach Gregory the Great; and though the Emperor might lie prostrate on the pavement of S. Ambrogio, paganism as an instinct was not yet dead, and Rome had not yet suffered all her afflictions. Worse things were in store for her, and there was to be even yet a great revulsion back to the old pagan faith. Spirituality was to win still another victory. But all this takes us to the next chapter in the person of Saint Augustine.

CHAPTER VI

WHEN on January 17, 395, the Emperor Theodosius
died, he left behind him as rulers his two sons, Arcadius
and Honorius, both of them already established on the
throne, Arcadius in the East, Honorius in the West.
The separation of the Empire into East and West, which
had been in practical existence for the last century, had
received its historical confirmation. Thus at the close of
the fourth century, the great event of the fifth century
was clearly foreshadowed, the separation of East and
West. But this separation was only a part of a more general break-up of the Empire, a break-up which was
caused by what we call the barbarian invasions. These
barbarian invasions, which were of course preparing the
way for modern Europe, and with which we shall be
dealing in all the three chapters which are left for us, are
of two distinct kinds, the general movement of the Teutonic peoples, which divides itself into the specific invasions of Visigoths, Vandals, Ostrogoths, Lombards, and
Franks, and which resulted in each case in a more or less
permanent settlement; and secondly, the marauding
invasions, notably that of the Huns.

But while these invasions tended to break up the Empire, they also rendered permanent the separation of the East from the West. The fact of this separation is very important, and the results of it are far-reaching. From the Western standpoint, in which we are of necessity interested, it was equivalent to the elimination of the Oriental elements which had come into the Empire. It was a renewal of the old distinction between Greece which faced east, and Rome which faced west. We see this best illustrated in the history of the Christian Church. The East is by nature given to philosophy and introspection, and thus we see the Eastern Church devoting its chief strength to the formation of creeds; but the Western world was essentially practical, hence the Western Church expended its energy in organization and disciplinary regulations.

But the effect of the separation reached even farther. Constantinople had taken precedence over Rome, she had absorbed the military strength of the Empire. The Western Empire was relatively unprotected. Thus for nine centuries Constantinople was able to protect herself, and thus spiritual and temporal dominion were kept distinct. But Rome was at the mercy of the barbarians, and while she stood at times theoretically under the protection of the Eastern Empire, this protection was a theory rather than a practice. Hence of necessity the spiritual power became engaged in temporal affairs, and the Holy Roman Empire came into existence. But in tracing the results of this separation we have gone far beyond the bounds of our fifth century, whither we must now return.

During the fifth century, in the Western Empire, to which we must confine ourselves, there was another struggle in progress, much more intense than that of Rome and the barbarians. It was the intellectual struggle between pagan and Christian thought. The physical struggle had ended. The series of edicts against pagan practices, which had emanated from the Christian emperors, had grown more and more severe, until they reached their culmination in the "nullus omnino" of Theodosius. "Let no man in any place in any city make sacrifice or worship the Lar with burnt offering or the Genius with wine or the Penates with perfumes, — let him light no lamp, burn no incense, hang no garlands" (*Cod. Theod.* XVI, 10, 12).

Be it never so well concealed, pagan sacrifice was becoming almost an impossibility. One was not safe even in the forests, and all that was left of it was what the Christian Church had itself adopted by compromise, and what was able to conceal itself in the churches themselves, and under the guise of Christian practice. It all comes to an end with a pathetic rapidity. The law books show us edict after edict, containing more and more detailed prohibitions of sacrifice, giving orders for the destruction of cult statues, commanding that the temples should be put to public uses, and that those in possession of them should be turned out. And that these edicts were no mere paper legislation, all our other sources prove clearly. Before the end of the century all the old priesthoods had disappeared, and all the references to Mithras and Magna Mater, which in 370 and 380 are so frequent, cease entirely. In many cases efforts were made to save the cult statues, and in certain cases they were crowned with success. Thus the formal expression of paganism was destroyed; and the fact that within a decade, Stilicho dared to burn the Sibylline Oracles, and met with no opposition, shows how thoroughly the work had been done.

But the intellectual struggle had grown all the more keen. The intense individualism of the early centuries, which had deprived Christianity of all political interest, was disappearing. In the presence of real physical danger from without, the dormant instincts of patriotism were being aroused. But with that mechanical association of ideas which characterizes the action of instincts, there came with the renaissance of patriotism, also the renaissance of pagan ideas in religion. We are fortunate in that we have in this fourth century a character, who not only exhibits in himself the struggle of pagan and Christian thought, but who does more than that, and after exhibiting the conquest of Christian thought, enters the field again to make easy for others the victory which he had obtained without human help. This is Augustine, the Bishop of Hippo. But to understand him and the forces with which he had to cope, we must first of all examine the political situation.

Our period covers sixty years (395–455), from the death of Theodosius to the capture of Rome by the Vandals. It includes the reigns of two emperors: of Honorius, the son of Theodosius, from 395 to 423; and of Valentinian III, 425 to 455. When Theodosius died, his son Honorius was, to be sure, only eleven years old, but he lived to be thirty-nine, and during the whole of his life failed to give the faintest indication of possessing a character or of being in any way conscious of the opportunities and responsibilities of life. He belonged to that class of useless rulers, whose absolute nonentity is only exaggerated by the prominence of the post which fate has given them.

But what Honorius lacked, his general Stilicho made good. The son of a Vandal chief, he brought a combination of unquestioned ability and doubtful devotion to the service of the Empire, and until his death (in 408) he was the real ruler. The events of Honorius's reign centre all of them in the invasion of the Visigoths. We must, therefore, say a word concerning the past history of these Visigoths.

The great Gothic nation had during the third and fourth centuries moved across Europe in a generally southerly direction, so that about the middle of the fourth century the Goths were settled in southern Russia. It was at this time, about 370, that the vanguard of the

Huns crossed into Europe. The coming of the Huns resulted in the separation of the Gothic nation into two
parts; that part which lay to the east, forever afterwards known to history as the Ostrogoths, and which
came into subjection to the Huns; and that part which
lay to the west, and whose inhabitants were forever
afterwards known as the Visigoths. In our present chapter we shall leave the Ostrogoths in subjection to the
Huns. The Huns are to rule over them for eighty years,
until, in 454, the Ostrogoths throw off the yoke; but that
belongs to the next chapter.

It is with the West Goths, the Visi-goths, that we have
now to do. At the approach of the Huns, these Visigoths
fled into the Roman Empire. A misunderstanding connected with their flight caused the Battle of Adrianople
(378), where the Emperor Valens lost his life. For seventeen years they remained as vassals of the Empire, until,
in 395, after the death of Theodosius, they chose Alaric
as their king. With the accession of their king Alaric,
the Visigoths step into history as a nation. They are no
longer a mere wandering horde of barbarians. They are
a united people with a definite purpose. They were destined eventually to lay the foundation of the greatness
of Spain, but for the present they contented themselves
with the invasion of Greece. Five years later, in 400,
Alaric led his nation into Italy. They came by way of
Belgrade, the valley of the Save, Laibach, and so over
the "Pear-Tree" Pass to Aquileia. They marched on Ra-

venna, but did not succeed in capturing it, and so turned northwest toward Milan. Meantime, terror had seized on the people of Rome, and many of the wealthier families were considering the advisibility of going to Corsica, or Sardinia, or southern France, a premature pilgrimage to Avignon! But in spite of Alaric's vision of "Penetrabis ad urbem" ("Thou shalt go even unto the City"), he did not as yet march upon Rome, and the inhabitants began to repair the walls, those walls which one hundred and thirty years before Aurelian had caused to be built.

In 404, the Emperor Honorius visited Rome for the purpose of celebrating there a triumph over the Visigoths. These later emperors did not love Rome, because Rome did not love them. But in spite of the lack of homage, the close approximation to disrespect which was always manifested toward them in Rome, sentiment demanded that they should return thither to celebrate the landmarks in their career. In connection with the celebration of this triumph, gladiatorial games were given in the Colosseum. These games afforded an opportunity for the performance of a deed worthy of the loftiest principles of Christianity. The contest had already begun, when, from the upper row of the spectators' seats, a figure was seen advancing, seat by seat, moving down toward the centre, and finally springing over the balustrade into the arena itself. There, amidst the breathless silence of the public, the man tried to separate the contestants. Then, as the multitude realized what he was attempting, that he was there to spoil their pleasure, the roar of the human beast burst forth, the man fell dead at the hands of the contestants, and the games proceeded. It was Telemachus, an Eastern monk, who had made this protest against the barbaric past. Christianity might indeed be called upon to respect ancient culture and to learn its lessons; but the new religion was ushering in a new world, in which all was not cruelty, in which the gain in humanity might offset something of the loss of culture. The sacrifice of Telemachus was not in vain, for Honorius shortly after decreed that gladiatorial games should cease.

The following year (405), Italy suffered from one of those marauding invasions, which are to be distinguished from the more orderly invasions, such as that of Alaric. About two hundred thousand men, under the leadership of a certain Radagaisus, started for Rome, and chose the route through the hills of Tuscany. It was there that Stilicho met and defeated them, and sold as slaves those of their army who were still alive. So numerous were they that they sold for an aureus — about fifteen francs — apiece; and even then the bargain was a poor one, because the captives were very likely to die, and the purchaser must pay the cost of burial.

After this brilliant victory of Stilicho, it is sad to learn that he was put to death three years later (408) as a traitor. But whether this act was just or not, it brought its own punishment, for there was no one to take his place, when in the same year Alaric began his second invasion of Italy. It was August when Stilicho was put to death at Ravenna, and now in September, Alaric and his army stood outside the walls of Rome; and the first siege began. Inside there is the story of famine and pestilence which was to become so familiar to Rome at intervals during more than a century to come. For a moment, like a flash of lightning in the dark, we have a vision of the depths of the popular religious consciousness. There is a renascence of paganism, a harking-back to the old instincts in the time of peril. A great longing arose among the people that certain magic rites should be performed by the *haruspices*. So strong did this feeling grow, that Pope Innocent (the First) gave his consent, adding the quaint reason that "he preferred the safety of the city to his own private opinion." But although the consent was given, there was no one who dared to perform the sacrifice.

Meantime negotiations for peace were being carried on, but the ambassadors were dealing with a hard taskmaster, who was so sure of himself that he could afford to jest with them. When they boasted that if Alaric did not make peace they might suddenly attack him with a great multitude, he answered them in a phrase which has become classic, a bit of Teutonic mother-wit, which seems as though it had stepped backwards out of the pages of Shakespeare, "The thicker the grass, the easier it is to mow."

He demanded all the gold, and all the silver, and all valuable movable property, and all slaves who were of barbarian origin; and when the Romans asked what they would have left, he answered "Your lives." But finally terms were obtained by which Rome paid five thousand pounds weight of gold, thirty thousand pounds weight of silver, four thousand robes of silk, three thousand hides dyed scarlet, and three thousand pounds of pepper.

Alaric now consented to retreat to the Danube provinces, there to establish his own kingdom under the nominal protectorate of Rome. We have no time to speculate on the amazing change in subsequent history which the fulfillment of this project would have portended. For the proposal was refused by Honorius, who, busied with his poultry farming at Ravenna, had no interest in Rome.

Thus, in the year 409, began the second siege of Rome, and the denouement was very curious. Instead of attacking Rome itself, Alaric captured Ostia, and so cut off Rome's supply of grain. The city soon came to terms, and appointed a joint emperor of Romans and Goths in the person of Attalus, who had been prefect of the city. We cannot enter into the fortunes of Attalus. Suffice to say that after a reign as short as it was impudent, and a failure which at one time came very close to being a success, he was deprived of his power and Honorius was relieved of his rival. But even then Alaric could make no peace with Ravenna, and so in 410, for a third time he took up the siege of the long-suffering city of Rome. But on this occasion some of the inhabitants preferred the mildness of Alaric to the inconveniences of a siege, and the Porta Salaria was opened to him during the night. Thus for the first time in eight hundred years, since the Gallic invasion of B.C. 390, Rome was entered by hostile troops. It is by no means easy to reach a decision as to the amount of damage done by the Goths. Tradition undoubtedly exaggerated its extent. But with the rise of German scholarship the tendency has all been in the opposite direction, until one is tempted to wonder whether they have not carried the defense of their ancestors to an unwarranted extent. Thus much is doubtless true, that the destruction of Rome, so far as its monuments and buildings are concerned, was not accomplished by the Goths and Vandals. It was the Renaissance itself which did most of the destructive work. But, on the other hand, the violent acts committed against persons, and the destruction and confiscation of movable property, were probably much greater than our modern authorities are willing to admit.

At the end of six days, Alaric and his people left Rome, marching southwards. There Alaric himself died in Calabria, and was buried under the waters of the river Busento. Then the Visigoths marched northwards, out of Italy and out of our story, except that we may add that they spent three years in Gaul and moved into Spain in 415, where in the course of the sixth century they renounced their Arian heresy and became Catholics, and in 711 were conquered by the Moors.

In 423 the parody on human life, which Honorius had been acting for thirty-nine years, was brought to a close by a fortunate attack of dropsy, and after a short period of usurpation Valentinian III, Placidia's seven-year-old son, became emperor, but Placidia, the daughter of Theodosius, reigned in his name.

At the beginning of this chapter we have seen how the Huns came out of Asia, how they settled in Russia, and how they caused the Gothic nation to break into two parts, the East or Ostro-Goths, whom they brought into subjection unto themselves, and the West or Visi-Goths, of whose history we have already briefly treated. The question of exactly who these Huns were has been much disputed. It has been thought that they were identical with the Hiung-Nu, against whom the Chinese built the great wall. Unfortunately the attractiveness of this suggestion is greater than its certainty, but it is at least possible. In any case, Ammianus Marcellinus has left us an accurate description of their appearance (XXXI, 2): —

They have all of them well-knit and strong limbs and fine necks. They are extremely ugly and terrible to behold, so that one would think them two-footed beasts, or like those roughly hewn stakes which are used for bridge railings. And although they do have a certain ugly resemblance to man, they are so uncivilized that they do not use fire or flavor their food, but they eat the roots of wild herbs and the half-raw meat of any sort of animal, meat which they warm up by placing it between their legs and the backs of their horses. They have no houses, and they avoid the shelter of roofs as they would the grave. For among them not even a cottage with a roof of reeds can be found. But wandering over the mountains and through the woods from their earliest childhood, they are accustomed to endure cold and hunger and thirst. And except in the most dire necessity they never go under a roof, and when they are indoors they never feel that they are safe. They wear linen garments or garments sewn together from the skins of field mice, and they have no change of garments, for example, for the house and for out of doors. But no matter how the color changes, the shirt which has once been put over the neck is not taken off or changed until by a long process of decay it has fallen into rags. They cover their heads with peaked caps; their hairy legs are clothed with goatskins, and their shoes are so shapeless as to prevent them from walking freely. And for this reason they are not well adapted to encounters on foot, but they perform their customary tasks, as it were, glued to their horses, which are hardy but ugly to look at, and which they sometimes ride woman-fashion. On horseback every man in this nation night and day buys and sells, takes food and drink, and bending over the slender neck of the horse falls into deep sleep and into the changeful panorama of dreams. And when a discussion is to take place upon important matters, it is on horseback that they all meet. They hold their discussions uncontrolled by kingly dignity, but, satisfied with the disorderly leadership of their chiefs, they interrupt with whatever comes into their minds. . . . No one of them plows or even touches a plow-handle. They all live without fixed abode. They wander abroad without home, without law, and without fixed rules of life, like those who are forever fugitives, together with their wagons in which they live, where their wives prepare for them their filthy garments and bear their children, and rear them until they are grown up. And if you ask one of them, he can never tell you where he came from, for he was conceived in one place, born far away from there, and brought up in a place still farther off; . . . like senseless animals, they are entirely ignorant of what is proper and improper; in their talk they are ambiguous and full of mystery. Nor are they ever moved by any regard for religion or superstition, but burning with a boundless passion for gold, they are so changeable and quick to wrath, that several times in the same day they grow angry with their comrades without reason, and make peace again without receiving any satisfaction.

How different our knowledge of Roman history would be, did Roman historians more often deign to draw such pen pictures.

In the year 433, after the Huns had been settled in Russia for more than sixty years, they chose Attila as their king, and under him they step into history. It is characteristic of these barbarian peoples that their prominence depends entirely upon the greatness of some one individual leader. Thus it is Alaric who leads the Visigoths into history, and Theodoric who leads the Ostrogoths, and Attila who leads the Huns.

Thus began a period of terror for Europe, which lasted no less than twenty years. In 451, Attila commenced his westward march. His army has been variously estimated, but it may well have contained several hundred thousand souls. It was indeed not so much an army as an aggregation of tribes and nations. We can follow their wanderings across the Rhine, to Metz, to Rheims, and so to

Paris, which was comforted by the assurances of Gené-
viève, but which really escaped because of its insignifi-
cance; and so on to Orléans, where they met with their
first rebuff. Turning eastward again, they found the
forces of Western civilization marshaled against them
on the Mauriac Plain, near Châlons-sur-Marne. There
the Huns and the Ostrogoths met Ætius with all the force
of Rome, including her allies, and among them the Visigoths. Thus the Gothic nation was divided against
itself, and that part of the nation which was later to
attempt so diligently the salvation of Rome was now
drawn up against her.

The battle was largely in favor of the Romans, but
they failed to destroy Attila and his forces, who continued the eastward march, which they had begun before
the battle. This march led them into Italy, where they
besieged Aquileia, and after desperate resistance captured and virtually destroyed the town. Then followed
the capture of Milan, and Attila's perpetration of his
grim jest. He found in the palace a picture portraying
the Emperor of Rome on the throne and the princes of
the East bowing before him. Attila did not destroy
the picture; he merely caused the actors to change places
so that the throne was occupied by the Eastern ruler,
while it was the Emperors of Rome who were bowing
before him.

The projected attack upon the city of Rome was prevented, partly by Attila's own superstitions, and partly

by the intervention of the venerable Pope Leo (the First). It is interesting to note that even at this early date, it is not the Emperor at Ravenna but the Pope at Rome who interests himself in the temporal salvation of the city.

One more great event must be attributed at least indirectly to Attila, the foundation of Venice. Terrified at his approach, the inhabitants of the villages on the mainland fled out into the marshes, that they might escape him. But they did not go out into the islands of the Adriatic, because the ships of the Vandals would have attacked them there. Thus, settling where there was in a sense neither land nor sea, they escaped the perils of both.

Shortly after this, Attila died, and his people were lost again in the East; but as he passes out of our picture we must pay him at least this tribute, that no man who ever lived has inspired so much fear in the human race. It was not only the terror of those who knew him when he was alive, but the terror which has radiated from him in his legendary capacity, all the way from Scandinavia to Burgundy. In the legend of Burgundy he is relatively well treated. There he is only the harmless hospitable Etzel of the *Niebelungenlied*. In Scandinavia he plots and schemes and murders in order to obtain the hidden treasure. But the fullness of his guilt is in the *Flagellum Dei*, the "Scourge of God," with which ecclesiastical tradition has invested him.

Thus for centuries Attila lived on, in the anathemas of the pulpit, and in the old-wives' tales of the nursery, while heretics and little children were urged to abandon the naughtiness of their ways in dread of him.

There remains still one chapter in our necessary historical review before we can turn to Augustine. In the fourth century another Teutonic people had been moving across Europe. This is the nation of the Vandals. In the year 330, we find them in Pannonia; in 406, they are settled in Gaul; three years later they are in Spain; and finally, in 428, possibly on the invitation of the traitor Boniface, they enter Africa, in the month of May, under the leadership of their king, Gaiseric. The Vandals, like the Visigoths, were Arians, not Catholics, but they had a religious zeal which the Visigoths lacked, and which caused them to engage in proselytism and religious persecution. Their conquest of Africa was, therefore, a sort of Holy War. In the year 430, they besieged the town of Hippo. We shall be speaking of this siege again in a few moments, but our interest will be inside rather than outside the walls. Nine years later they captured Carthage, and it was there that their king, Gaiseric, received the message of the widowed empress, Eudoxia, asking for his aid. They did not wait on the order of their going, and the fleet arrived at Ostia with all possible speed. Then followed the journey up the Tiber, and soon they stood before the gates of Rome. Again the Pope, the same great Leo, interceded in behalf of Rome, and obtained such guaranties as he might; and then the pillage began. For fourteen days Rome was plundered, and then the heavily laden galleys sailed away on the homeward journey to Carthage. It is a melancholy testimony to the wealth of Rome that at this, her third plundering, there was still an abundance of riches left.

It was necessary that we should spend this time on things that may well seem remote from our subject, in order that we might create at once a background and an atmosphere. If the fourth century had been, in the main, a period of exultant triumph for Christianity, this first half of the fifth century was a period of deep religious depression. The end of the world was coming, but not in the way the early church had hoped for. There was no indication of the Millennium, and the clouds in the sky did not usher in triumphantly the second coming of the Lord; and the elect were not caught up to be forever with him. There were clouds enough in the sky of life, but they were full of the arrows that fly by night, and of the pestilence that stalketh at noonday. Human life had no peace; and, when there were no wars, there were rumors of war. Visigoths, Huns, Vandals, — they had all threatened the peace of Rome, and two nations had utterly despoiled her. It was the dark before the dawn of Theodoric, the Ostrogoth, but men had no good reason to expect a dawn. The other way of salvation, the abandonment of this wicked world and the embrace of monasticism, was only at its beginning. The majority of men still stayed in the world, but it was a sad place. Above all things, thinking men sought for an explanation; they sought for it with an intensity into which we in our relatively happy world can scarcely enter; an intensity that our own world has, however, seen in the person of Tolstoy. They had almost all the modern paraphernalia of thought, with the exception of Immanuel Kant. The unsolvable problems of the world are as old as the world itself, and the material for solution grows very little through the centuries. There were still the same three schools of thought that men had used a century before. Mithraism as a religion was dead, but Manichæanism, the doctrines of the disciples of Mani, was its legitimate successor. Neoplatonism in its serenity was practically unchanged, as it is in a sense even to the present day. Perhaps Christianity alone had been developing, but it had as yet made no great progress. These were the only available solutions to the problem of life.

The character which we have chosen, hoping to see, in his inner life, the reflection of the inner life of his age, is Aurelius Augustinus, better known to the world as St. Augustine. I have chosen him, first, because he was a rounded man, drinking in to the full the life of his day, and hence knowing human life as only such a one can; and secondly, because we are so well informed regarding the events of his inner and his outer life. For the formative period of that life, the first thirty-three years, we have one of the greatest of all human documents, his own *Confessions*, a book by the love of which we may measure the depth of our life.

Augustine was born at Tagaste, in Numidia, on the thirteenth of November, 354. His father, Patricius, was a man of some prominence, a Decurio of the town, and a good example of a cheerful, healthy, well-fed pagan; his mother, Monnica, was all that a good mother should be, and there is no higher place that any woman can hold. If we are at all to appreciate Augustine, we must follow the story of his life from its beginnings as he tells it to us himself. I shall have occasion to quote frequently from the *Confessions*, and in so doing I shall make use of the translation of Canon Bigg. His translation is so beautiful that it would be folly to try to rival it.

In the opening chapters of the first book we have a most extraordinary series of passages regarding Augustine's babyhood. For example (1, 6):—

Yet suffer me to speak before Thy mercy, me who am but dust and ashes. . . . For what is it that I would say, O Lord my God, save that I know not whence I came hither into this dying life, shall I call it, or living death? And the comforts of Thy pity received me, as I have heard from the father and mother of my flesh, from whom and in whom Thou didst fashion me in time: for I do not recollect. And so the comfort of human milk was ready for me. For my mother and my nurses did not fill their own bosoms, but Thou, O Lord, by their instrumentality gavest me the food of infancy . . . for of a truth all goods come from Thee, O God; and from my God is all my health. This I learned afterwards, when Thou didst call loudly to me by all Thy benefits, within me and without.

For in those days I could but suck and feel pleasure and weep at fleshly pain, nothing more. Afterwards I began also to smile, at first in sleep, then awake. For this I have been told and believe, since I see other babies do the same But I do not recollect how it was with myself.

And from this quaint touch he turns and cries, not as an inquiring metaphysician, but as a human being longing for knowledge: —

Tell me, I beseech Thee, O God . . . tell me whether another life of mine died before my infancy began or only that which I spent in the womb of my mother? . . . Even before this, what was there, O my God? — Was I anywhere? Was I any one? . . . Whence came so wondrous a creature but from Thee, O Lord? Can any one make himself? Can the stream of being and of life that runs into us derive from any other fountain? No; Thou hast made us, O Lord, whose being and whose life are ever the same, because Thou art nothing else than supreme being, supreme life. . . . How many days of mine and of my father's have passed through Thy to-day, from Thy eternity received their mode of being and existed after their fashion!

One of the extraordinary characteristics of the *Confessions* is the ease of transition. We are forever changing altitude, now up, now down, but we feel no shock of abrupt change, and yet in the text itself there are no attempts at artificial bridges of transition. The processes of accommodation are in the writer himself, because he is following his own moods; and just because he is able to express himself with absolute naturalness, the reader shares his moods, and thus makes all the changes, not as a spectator, but as a man of like passions with Augustine, living out with him and in himself the experiences described for him. Thus, a chapter or two later, we find it quite natural that Augustine should be talking simply of the processes of education, beginning with the baby's attempts to learn to speak (1, 8): —

Thus gradually I acquired a store of words arranged in sentences, and by frequent repetitions, I came to perceive of what things they were the symbols, and by training my mouth to their utterance, I gained the power of verbal expression. So I exchanged with those about me the symbols of meaning, and launched out upon the stormy sea of human fellowship, while still depending upon the authority of parents and the direction of elders.

His experience of studying the classics is that of many another boy (1, 13): —

But even now I cannot understand why I hated Greek, which I was taught in my earliest school-days. For I loved Latin — the literature, I mean, not the grammar. For the first lessons of the Latin schools, in which one learns to read, write, and multiply, I thought as dull and penal as Greek.

And again (1, 14): —

Why did I hate my Greek literature, which was full of such songs? For Homer also weaves these fables with a skillful hand, nor is any vanity so delightful as his. Yet he was distasteful to me as a boy, and so, I think, would Virgil be to Greek boys, if they were compelled to learn him in the same way, that is to say, by dint of drudgery.

It is this extraordinary humanity which characterized the real Augustine throughout all his life. There is the marvelous chapter on the blessings of boyhood, the sheer physical joy of being a boy (I, 20): —

O Lord, my God, Thou best and most excellent Creator and Ruler of the world, I should owe Thee thanks, even though Thou hadst wished that I should never be more than a boy. For I was, I was alive, I could feel, I could guard my personality, the imprint of that mysterious unity from which my being was derived — surely every part of such a creature calls for wonder and praise. But all this is the bounty of my God, and not my own, and all these capacities are good, and I am the sum of them. Truly, then, He who made me is good and very good, and to Him will I give loud thanks for all the good that belonged to me even as a boy.

In the second book we pass to his youth, that youth which was to mean so much to his later life. And if he seems to brood over the ill-spent years more than we feel they deserve, we should remember that we know Monnica only through him; and the pain that arose from the thought of the grief which he had caused her is his own pain, that incomparable pain of having caused sorrow to her who bore us. And even if in this mood the stealing of apples seems a proof of original sin, there is a wonderful charm in the psychological analysis (II, 4): "For I stole what I had in plenty, and much better. What I wanted to enjoy was not the thing I stole, but the actual sin of theft."

In 371, when he was seventeen, his father, "who was but a poor burgess — with a spirit beyond his purse" (II, 3), managed to afford the expense of sending him to

Carthage to study to become a rhetorician, to Carthage "where debauchery bubbled like a frying-pan" (III, 1), and where he sought something to love, "loving the idea of love, and hating the tranquil path where there are no mousetraps." It was in Carthage that he "polluted the brook of friendship with the sewage of lust."

It was at this time that the stage bewitched him. "Why," he cries (III, 2), "do men desire to be saddened by the representations of tragic misfortunes which they do not in the least desire to suffer?" "Yet the spectator does desire to be saddened by them, and the sadness is the very pleasure that he seeks. Surely this is wretched folly." We need no more than this to see why Augustine did not love Greek. We are very far from the Aristotelian "Catharsis" of emotion by the exhibition of passion.

It was scarcely to be expected that this modest, introspective youth would be popular with his fellow students.

I would take no part [he says (III, 3)] in the wild doings of the "Wreckers," a cruel and devilish name, which was looked upon as the stamp of the best set. I lived amongst them, feeling a kind of impudent shame, because I could not keep pace with them. I went about with them, and of some of them I made friends; yet I always disliked their way of going on, their "wreckings," their wanton attacks upon the shyness of freshmen, and the unprovoked affronts with which they carried on their malignant amusement. Nothing could be more like the conduct of devils, and what name could be fitter for them than "Wreckers"?

Meantime he was absorbed in his work, in no mechanical spirit, but with an ambition for outward success, when he chanced upon Cicero's treatise *Hortensius*, and the rhetoric was suddenly forgotten in the message of the book itself (III, 4): —

Among such comrades, in those years of indiscretion, I was studying books of rhetoric, wherein I desired to excel, seeking through the joys of vanity a flashy and reprobate success, and in the usual course I had entered upon a book by one Cicero, whose tongue all men admire though not his heart. It was the *Hortensius*, a treatise in which he extols the study of philosophy. That book changed my mind, changed my very prayers to Thee, O Lord, and altered my wishes and aspirations. From that moment vain hopes ceased to charm, and with a strange and heartfelt passion I began to long for the immortality of wisdom. Thenceforth began my upward way and my return towards Thee. . . . How did I burn, O my God, how did I burn to soar away from earth to Thee.

Thus Augustine became a philosopher and began his quest of the truth, a quest which occupied more than sixteen years of his life, and led him through the whole circle of ancient religious thought. The great questions, Who am I? Why am I? filled his mind and would not leave him. Again and again he tried in vain to abandon the search.

As the first step in this search, he fell among the Manichees, and became an auditor of their doctrines. The rest of the third book, all of the fourth, and a portion of the fifth, are devoted to a refutation of Manichæanism, a refutation which was by no means difficult. In 375, at the age of twenty-one, he became a teacher of rhetoric in his own native town of Tagaste, and afterwards a teacher of legal rhetoric at Carthage. Of his life in Carthage he says (IV, 2): "In these years I lived with one not joined to me in lawful wedlock, upon whom my vagabond foolish passion had settled, yet with but one, and I was faithful to her." These were anxious years for Monnica, but her faith did not waver. Once she dreamed that she was standing alone, when some one came and stood beside her, and looking up she saw that it was her son. She interpreted her dream to mean that Augustine would become a Christian. He himself accepted the dream, but said that they would be together in belief, when she herself became a Manichee. Then she answered, without a moment's hesitation (III, 11): "No, he did not say where he is, you will be, but where you are, he will be"; an answer at which Augustine confesses himself more impressed than at the dream itself. There is, too, such a modern note, but modern only because it is eternal, in the bishop's words (III, 12): "It cannot be that the son of these tears should be lost."

In 383, after eight years of teaching in Africa, and being now twenty-nine years of age, he received a call to a professorship at Rome. The boisterousness of the students at Carthage, the "Wreckers," with whom he had never sympathized, made him ready to go.

. . . At Carthage [he says (v, 8)], there is a disgraceful license of disorder along the students. They burst shamelessly into the room, and with the demeanor of madmen break up the discipline which the teacher has established for the better progress of his pupils. Many things they will do with the utmost effrontery which are real outrages, punishable by law, if it were not that custom has sanctioned them, a custom which proves them the more unhappy, because it allows them to do what Thy eternal law never will allow. And they think that they act thus with impunity, though the very blindness with which they act is their punishment, and they suffer infinitely more harm than they inflict. So it came to pass, that, as a teacher, I was compelled to endure in others the evil habits which, as a student, I had refused to adopt; and on this account I was glad to remove to a place where, as I was assured by men who knew, such conduct was not tolerated.

His mother was opposed to his going to Rome, but by a disgraceful ruse he deceived her and set sail. This is one of the few passages where we feel a curious hardness, which may in its turn explain some of his theological views. "Thus I lied to my mother, and such a mother!" But then the thought comforts him that in going to Rome he had been unwittingly going to be converted (v, 8): —

And what was she beseeching of Thee, O my God, with all these tears, but that Thou wouldst prevent me from sailing? But Thou, in Thy hidden wisdom, didst grant the substance of her desire, yet refuse the thing she prayed for, in order that thou mightest effect in me what she was ever praying for.

And then, with a touch reminiscent of the Æneid: —

The wind blew and filled our sails, and the shore receded from our gaze. There was she in the morning, with wild sorrow, besieging Thine ears with complaints and sighs which

Thou didst not regard, for by my desires Thou wast drawing me to the place where I should bury my desires and her carnal yearning was being chastened by the scourge of grief. For she loved to keep me with her, as mothers are wont, yes, far more than most mothers, and she knew not what joy Thou wert preparing for her out of my desertion.

The whole passage is a curious mixture of the theologian and the loving son, and it is only fair to add that this is one of the few passages in the *Confessions* where the theologian dominates the man.

But his Roman experiences were not successful. He describes them to us, with admirable frankness (v, 12):

I began diligently to apply myself to the object that had brought me to Rome, the teaching of the art of rhetoric. And first I gathered at my house a little company of scholars, to whom and by whom I was beginning to be known; when, lo, I discovered that there were vexations at Rome from which I had been free in Africa. It was true, as appeared, that young profligates did not practice "wreckings" here, but "all of a sudden," said my friends, "a number of them will enter into a plot to escape paying their fees, and march off to another teacher," breaking their faith and despising justice for love of money.

And so [he continues (v, 13)], when the Milanese sent to Rome, requesting the Prefect of the city to provide them with a teacher of Rhetoric, and to furnish him for the journey at the public expenses, I made application, through those very Manichæan fanatics, from whom my going was to detach me, though neither they nor I foresaw this result, to Symmachus, who was the Prefect, desiring him that upon due examination, I might have the post. So I came to Milan, where I found the Bishop Ambrose.

I have gone thus into detail in recounting the history of Augustine's life up to the turning-point, for two reasons. I have wanted you to know him as the marvelously human character that he is, and not as the theologian, pure and simple, and in the second place, it seemed worth while to contrast the quiet tenor of his outward life with the events of his day. We think of these years as anything but peaceful. In the year that Augustine was born, Gallus was being entrapped and put to death at Pola, and Julian imprisoned at Milan. While Augustine was learning to talk and read, the whole tragedy of Julian's life was being enacted. When he began to study at Carthage, the Huns were breaking into Russia; in the year when he moved to Rome, the Emperor Gratian was killed; and now when he reaches Milan, Ambrose is in the midst of his controversy with Justina.

Next to his relationship to his mother, his relation to Ambrose is the most beautiful thing in Augustine's life.

So I came to Milan [he says (v, 13)], where I found the Bishop Ambrose, Thy godly servant, known throughout the world as one of the best of men, whose eloquent discourses were at that time diligently supplying to Thy people the fatness of Thy wheat, the gladness of Thy oil, and the sober intoxication of Thy wine. By Thee was I led blindly to him, that by him I might be led with open arms to Thee. That man of God received me as a father, and welcomed the stranger like a true bishop. And I began to love him, not at first as a teacher of the truth, which I despaired of finding in Thy church, but as a fellow creature who was kind to me. I listened attentively to his sermons, not with the right attitude of mind, but criticizing his eloquence, — whether it was equal to his reputation, whether its stream was broader or narrower than men reported. Thus I hung eagerly upon his expressions, while as regards his subject, I remained a cool and contemptuous looker-on, delighted only with the charm of his style.

We see his love of Ambrose growing as we turn the pages.

I could not ask him what I wanted, as I wanted, because the shoals of busy people, to whose infirmities he ministered, came between me and his ear and lips. And in the few moments when he was not thus surrounded, he was refreshing either his body with needful food, or his mind with reading. . . . Often when we attended (for the door was open to all, and no one was announced), we saw him reading silently, but never otherwise, and often sitting for some time without speaking (for who would presume to trouble one so occupied?), we went away again.

It is well for us to remember this picture of the silent scholar and the timid spectator, when we think of Ambrose only as the proud churchman who humbled Theodosius, and of Augustine as the theologian of the sinfulness of infants.

It was at this time that he and some of his friends contemplated a peaceful life away from the crowd (VI, 14):—

With a band of friends I had been discussing and deploring the stormy anxieties of human life, and by this time we had almost decided to live a peaceful life away from the crowd. Peace we thought we might obtain by clubbing together whatever means we possessed, and so making one common stock; in the sincerity of friendship there was to be no mine or thine, but all were to have one purse and the whole was to belong to each and all. We thought we might reckon some ten members of the fraternity, of whom some were very wealthy, especially Romanianus, my fellow townsman, whom at this time pressing anxieties of business had brought up to the Bounty Office. From childhood he had been one of my nearest friends. He was the warmest advocate of our project, and his words carried great weight, because his wealth was much greater than that of the others. We had resolved that each year two of us should be managers, and provide all that was needful, while the others enjoyed complete leisure. But as soon as we began to ask whether the wives, whom some already had, and I hoped to have, would tolerate this, our excellent plan burst to pieces in our hands, and was cast aside like a broken thing.

In these months the hold of Manichæanism was broken, but as its coarse dualism became more and more repugnant to him, the doctrines of Neoplatonism made a stronger and stronger appeal; and so he begins a comparative study of Neoplatonism and Christianity. We have already anticipated that study in our chapter on the origins of Christianity, and we need not go into it again. It was the humility of Christianity and its personal note, which made their strong appeal. Of Neoplatonism he says (VII, 20): "Where was that charity which buildeth upon the foundation of humility?" And again: "No one there [in Neoplatonism] hearkens to Him that calleth, 'Come unto me all ye that labour.'"

These were the days when Ambrose was holding the basilica against Justina, and teaching the people the antiphonal chants (IX, 7): —

The people of God were keeping ward in the church, ready to die with Thy servant, their Bishop. Among them was my mother, living unto prayer, and bearing a chief part in that anxious watch. Even I myself, though as yet untouched by the fire of Thy spirit, shared in the general alarm and distraction. Then it was that the custom arose of singing hymns and psalms, after the use of the Eastern provinces, to save the people from being utterly worn out by their long and sorrowful vigils.

His own struggles grow more and more intense until the summit of his anguish is reached one memorable day, when he went out into the garden attached to his lodgings to meditate and pray. Then occurred one of those strange hearings of voices, which are so characteristic of those days, occurring as the stories do in the lives of Alaric, Ambrose, Augustine, and many others.

Lo, I heard a voice [VIII, 12] from a neighboring house. It seemed as if some boy or girl, I knew not which, was repeating in a kind of chant the words, "Take and read, take and read." Immediately, with changed countenance, I began to think intently whether there was any kind of game in which children sang those words; but I could not recollect that I had ever heard them. I stemmed the rush of tears and rose to my feet; for I could not think but that it was a divine command to open the Bible and read the first passage I lighted upon. . . . I ran back to the place where Alypius was sitting; for when I quitted him I had left the volume of the Apostle lying there. I caught it up and opened it, and read in silence the passage on which my eyes first fell, "Not in rioting and drunkenness, not in chambering and wantonness, not in strife and envying; but put ye on the Lord Jesus Christ, and make not provision for the flesh to fulfill the lusts thereof." No further would I read, nor was it necessary. As I reached the end of the sentence, the light of peace seemed to be shed upon my heart, and every shadow of doubt melted away.

Thereupon he decided to resign his professorship of rhetoric; but with a laudable desire to escape publicity, he waited until the vintage holidays before carrying out his resolve. Then follows the retreat to the country-house of his friend Verecundus, at Cassicium, until in the next year (387) at Easter, he was baptized by Ambrose at Milan. Then, accompanied by Monnica, he set out to return to Africa.

As the day drew near [IX, 10] on which she was to depart from this life, Thou knewest it though we did not, it fell out, as I believe, through the secret workings of Thy providence, that she and I were leaning by ourselves on the ledge of a window, from which we looked down on the garden of our house. Yonder it was in Ostia by Tiber, where, away from the crowd, fatigued by the long journey from Milan, we were recruiting ourselves for the sea voyage. Sweet was the converse we held together, as forgetting those things which were behind, and reaching forth unto those things which were before, we asked ourselves in the presence of Thee, the Truth, what will be the manner of that eternal life of the saints, which eye hath not seen, nor ear heard, neither hath it entered into the heart of man.

The picture is beautiful, but not the least beautiful part is its framework, because it is so typically Italian, with its standing by the window, so thoroughly modern in touch.

Within five days Monnica was "seized by a fever,"

and as she lay dying, far from her native land of Africa, yet on the point of setting sail for home, she said: —

Lay this body where you will, and be not anxious about it. Only I beseech you remember me at the altar of God, wherever you are. . . . Nothing is far from God. There is no fear that at the end of the world He will not know whence to summon me.

And so we part with the *Confessions*, repeating Augustine's own prayer (IX, 13): —

May she rest in peace, therefore, with her husband, her first and only husband, whom she obeyed, bringing forth fruit unto Thee with patience, that she might gain him also unto Thee. And do Thou inspire, O Lord my God, do Thou inspire Thy servants, my brethren, Thy sons, my masters, whom I serve with heart and voice and pen, that whoso reads these pages may remember before Thy altar Monnica, Thy handmaid, and Patricius, once her husband, through whose flesh Thou didst bring me into this life, I know not how. Let them remember with godly love those who were my parents in this transitory life, those who were my brethren under Thee, our Father, in the Catholic mother, those who are my fellow citizens in the Eternal Jerusalem, for which Thy people of pilgrims yearn from their going-out until their coming home again. So shall her dying request be granted her in richer abundance by the prayers of many through my *Confessions* rather than through my prayers.

For the remaining forty-three years of Augustine's life (for he died at the age of seventy-six), we have no such wealth of material, but the main facts are clear. He returned to Africa immediately, and during the next ten years came the actual writing of the *Confessions*. In

391, he was made Presbyter of Hippo, and then Bishop, an office which he held for thirty-four years. These years of his bishopric were years of great theological productivity, in which so many streams of later theological discussion have their rise, that the most diverse sects find to their chagrin that they meet in him. Fortunately we have no cause to go into these things, and we can but quote Gibbon: "My personal acquaintance with the Bishop of Hippo does not extend beyond the *Confessions* and the *City of God*."

In 430, while the Vandals were besieging Hippo, the aged Bishop, knowing that his life was soon to end, and true to his principle that, when possible, a man should spend the closing days of his life in penitence, retired to his room and for ten days meditated upon the penitential psalms of David. Thus died Augustine.

If the *Confessions* have taught us to know the man personally, it is the *City of God* which brings him into our story, and connects him with the general history of Roman religious consciousness.

We have seen that Christianity came into the world as a religion of the Jews, we have also seen that Paul extended it to include the Gentiles. In a word, it became coterminal with the Roman Empire. When under Constantine it became the religion of the Roman state, this national idea of Christianity was emphasized still more strongly. Therefore, in the minds of the great majority of those who lived in the last half of the fourth century and in the first half of the fifth century, Christianity was a national religion. Such instincts of patriotism as were still left to them attempted to exercise themselves under Christian forms. But there were great difficulties in finding suitable forms, and the instinct of patriotism found expression much more readily in the old religion which was now prohibited.

All that was necessary to produce a revival of the old religion was that the national consciousness should receive a severe shock. Such a shock it did receive in the capture of Rome by the Visigoths. After remaining unconquered for eight hundred years, Rome had been forced to open her gates to the enemy. For seven hundred of these years Jupiter Optimus Maximus had protected her successfully; and now, within a century of the acceptance of the Christian God, she had fallen. Christianity, therefore, as a national religion was a failure.

And with the fall of Rome, patriotism itself received a stupendous impulse, so that once again men felt that religion was to be judged by its practical effects on the nation. Then it was that Augustine, questioned by some converts, conceived the idea of writing a treatise on *The City of God*. As often happens when men attempt very great things, the conception is better than the execution; and in this case the title is much more inspiring than the work itself. It would, indeed, be an easy matter to prove that it was the Romans themselves, and not their gods, who had been the defenders of Rome during these centuries, and now in the moment of weakness it was not God, but the Romans, who had failed. But this is not sufficient, nor is it the original feature of the work. Many others before Augustine, for example, Ambrose, had argued after this fashion.

But his thought goes infinitely higher. Christianity is not a national religion. Its primary object is not the glory and the power of the city of Rome. But there are two cities forever separate: the city of Rome, the city of the world, and the city of God, "cuius fundamenta sunt in montibus sacris."

Christianity is not dependent on any earthly city. Its duration is not contemporaneous with Rome. Rome may fall, but the city of God abideth forever. This was the answer of Augustine to those who saw in the capture of Rome by the Visigoths the proof of the failure of Christianity. It was not said in any spirit of hostility to Rome; nay, the whole line of thought was suggested and brought into being by a great love of that city. It was also, if you will, a strange prophecy of the ultimate separation of church and state, a free church in a free state. But for the present it was one of those grand ideas which are so much in advance of their time that they lie dormant for centuries. By the strange vicissitudes of history the repeated humiliation of Rome was to make her par excellence the sacred city of the Western world. For a millennium and a half the city of Rome was to become more and more synonymous in men's minds with the City of God. From this fact were to come great gains to civilization and religion. And it would not be at all wonderful if even in our own day Rome should recover the universality of her dominion. But this is possible only along the line, which Augustine has pointed out, that it is the spiritual city, the City of God, which abideth forever.

CHAPTER VII

BENEDICT AND THE OSTROGOTHS: THE PROBLEM OF THE
SALVATION OF ANCIENT CULTURE

CHRISTIANITY had stood the shock of the capture of
Rome. It was not only the capture by the Visigoths,
while Augustine was still alive; but after his death had
come the Vandals. The new religion might therefore
feel itself secure, at least in name. Its foes from henceforth were to be those of its own household. But with
ancient culture the problem was not so simple. A century before, Julian, with a farsightedness for which he
has not always been given credit, had divined the problem of the difficulty of conserving ancient culture. From
his standpoint culture and religion were inseparable;
hence he tried, on the one hand, to restore ancient religion, and, on the other hand, to preserve ancient culture by prohibiting the teaching of pagan literature by
Christians. His solution was a failure, but he deserves
the credit of having realized the problem. During the
century since Julian's death, we find no further attempt
made to solve the difficulty. Yet, like many difficult
problems, it was growing more difficult with every year
of delay. With the beginning of the barbarian invasions
a new kind of destructive agency commenced its work.
Hitherto this ancient culture had suffered merely by

neglect, by a negative force, but now it is menaced by the positive force of hostile destruction.

Fortunately, at the close of the fifth century and at the beginning of the sixth century, the period with which we are to deal in this chapter, two earnest attempts are made to save this precious heritage. One of these attempts, which seemed to promise success, proved to be a failure; the other, whose issue seemed doubtful, was centuries later crowned with success. The two leaders of these movements probably never met; and very probably one of them never heard the name of the other. They are Theodoric and Benedict.

Theodoric's attempt is involved in the establishment of an Ostrogothic kingdom in Italy, which was to respect and preserve the things of Rome; Benedict's attempt was the regulation of the already existing tendencies to monasticism, so that the monasteries themselves might be the preservers of ancient culture.

Had Theodoric's attempt succeeded, we should have had a virtually unbroken Roman tradition; but to offset that, we should have had no Holy Roman Empire, and therefore no centralizing power in the world of Europe. Instead, thanks to Benedict's success, while the tradition was broken in the world at large, it was preserved in the monasteries, and received a universal fruition at the time of the Renaissance.

Cognizant of much that we have lost, and deeply regretting that loss, we still feel that Fate has chosen for

us the better part. Our task in this chapter is the consideration of these two attempts.

The possibility of a great Gothic empire in Russia
was destroyed by the coming of the Huns. We have
seen how the advent of these strange Orientals caused
the Gothic empire to break into two parts, — a western section, the Visigoths, with whose history we have
already dealt, and an eastern section, the Ostrogoths,
who form the subject of the first part of our present
chapter.

It was about the year 370 that these Ostrogoths were
brought into subjection by the Huns, whom they continued to serve for more than eighty years. We have seen
the proof of their devotion or at least of the thoroughness
of their subjection, in their participation in the Battle of
the Mauriac Plain, where they fought on the side of the
Huns against their brethren, the·Visigoths. Jordanes,
their historian, apologizes for the action of the Ostrogoths on this occasion, excusing it on the ground of their
absolute subjection. In the main, however, the yoke
of the Huns was relatively light. Nevertheless, after
Attila's death, when the Hunnish power had been
broken, they succeeded in obtaining their independence
by the Battle of Nedao. On the day when the news of
this great national victory reached the palace of their
king, the queen brought forth a man-child, who was
called Theodoric, "Thiuda-Reiks," the "people-ruler."
This baby was destined to form a great Gothic king-

dom, and almost to succeed in the task of preventing the existence of the "Middle Ages."

When Theodoric was seven years old (461), he was sent as a hostage to Constantinople, where he found favor in the sight of the Emperor Leo, being, as Jordanes says, "puerolus elegans." For ten years he lived at Constantinople, participating in the luxuries of the life of a king's son, who was a hostage for his people. But these ten years were not able to sap the strength of his Northern energy, for at the expiration of the time, being now a youth of seventeen, he returned home, and finding his father absent, collected a band of ten thousand young men, the old Teutonic *comitatus* of which Tacitus speaks, and conducted an expedition against the Sarmatians. Having captured Belgrade, he returned home rejoicing. He had won his spurs and had now a right to sit among the leaders.

There now follows a difficult period in his life, a long stretch of seventeen years, as long as the span of life which he had already covered, for he was but seventeen. It was a period of vacillation and indecision. Constantinople and his own people both called him. Should he be willing to leave his people, an honorable and comfortable career awaited him at Constantinople, but to do this would be in a sense to deny his own royalty. If he abode with his people, he would be indeed their king, but life would be one long struggle against starvation, and the oppression by the Empire. Finally his decision is made.

Be the cost never so great, he will stand by his people. Then the suggestion arises that his people might be led into a new land, even the land of Italy. In the vicissitudes of the latter half of the fifth century this land of Italy had fallen away from the Empire, and had come into the power of a foreign tyrant, and a band of mercenaries. This tyrant was Flavius Odovacar, who with the Herulians had been undisputed master of Italy since 476, when he had deposed Romulus Augustulus. There was need that Italy should be recaptured for the Empire.

It is not exactly clear who originated this idea of invading Italy for the purpose of recapturing it for the Empire, but it seems most likely that it came from Theodoric himself. There is also some uncertainty as to the exact nature of the contract into which Theodoric entered with the Emperor Zeno. But the spirit of the contract seems to have been that Theodoric was to rule in Italy in case he captured it, but he was to rule in the name of the Emperor.

Thus, in the late autumn of 488, Theodoric started. We must not conceive of his forces as that of an army in marching trim. They resembled rather a nation, for every man brought his family with him. The women and the children lived in wagons, and the flocks and the herds were driven with them. It has been estimated that there were perhaps two hundred thousand souls in all, but four fifths of these were noncombatants, so that the fighting force would not have exceeded forty thousand.

For the first three hundred miles their journey was easy. Then they came into the territory of the Gepidæ, through whom they had to fight their way, a tedious process, consuming the winter, the spring, and part of the summer of 488–89. The Gepidæ were defeated in numerous conflicts, especially in the Battle of Ulca, and in August, 489, they began the descent into Italy, across the Julian Alps, and over the "Birnbaum" Pass. Within two months Theodoric had inflicted two severe defeats on the tyrant Odovacar, one at Isonzo on August 28, and one at Verona on September 30. Odovacar fled for refuge to Ravenna, while Theodoric advanced on Milan.

Ennodius, in his *Panegyric* on Theodoric, recounts an incident which throws light on the personality of Theodoric at this time. He tells us that before the Battle of Verona, Theodoric addressed his mother and his sister as follows: —

Thou knowest, O mother, that thy fame is spread throughout all the world because of the honor of thine offspring, because on the day of my birth, thou didst bring forth a man-child. And now the time has come when the field of battle shall declare what manner of son thou hast. There is work to be done with the sword, that the glory of my ancestors may lose nothing through me. For how does the glory of our fathers profit us, unless we are aided by our own? There stands before my eyes my father, of whom the fortune of battle never made sport, who made Fortune favorable to him by the might which demanded success. That was, indeed, a leader under whom to fight! — who had no fear of wavering omens, but compelled them to be favorable. Bring forth the embroidered garments, the ornaments of the loom. Let me be more finely clad in the line of battle than ever I was on a holiday. Let him who does not know me by my charge, recognize me by my splendor. And let the glory of my garments attract the eyes of the covetous, and if I am wounded, let me present a fairer sight. Let him have a reward of his labors, him to whom thou, O Fortune, shall give my throat. And let those who did not have the opportunity of beholding me fighting, gaze wondering upon my splendor as I lie there.

As Ennodius addressed these words directly to Theodoric himself, it is scarcely likely that they are the invention of Ennodius. Thus they present a marvelous picture of the boastful Northerner, the impetuous Goth; and at the same time they offer a presage of those mediæval days of *tournées* and embroidered garments, which were so soon to come.

After this brilliant opening campaign, the progress of Theodoric's conquest became slower. It was almost a year before the next considerable victory, the Battle of the Adda, August 11, 490. The war could, however, be ended only by the capture of Ravenna, and the taking prisoner of Odovacar. It was a tedious blockade, and the city did not surrender until February 25, 493, in the fourth year of the siege. In Theodoric's case, as in that of Augustus, the beginning and the end of his career were not free from stain, while the main portion of his reign was unimpeachable; and the murder of Cicero was as ignoble, if not as brutal, an act as the slaying of Odovacar. The revolting feature of it in Theodoric's case is the fact that Theodoric's own hand committed the murder, and that Odovacar was his guest at the time.

In spite of this brutal prolusion and an almost equally bloody epilogue, Theodoric's reign was almost perfect. Conscious that he was ruling over two peoples, Goth and Romans, he established a federation, but avoided the dangers and difficulties of attempts at fusion. Doubtless he looked forward to the time when such a fusion would be possible, but he realized its impracticability for the present. His great object was the preservation of that which he called CIVILITAS, which was nothing more or less than ancient culture. He strove constantly to be impartial, and, mindful perhaps of the murdered Odovacar, he cultivated self-restraint. This mildness was particularly noticeable in religious matters, where we should have expected him to be otherwise; for he was an Arian, and not a Catholic, and might well have shared in the Arian's love of persecution. The outward events of his reign are few, just in proportion to the peaceful character of it. His capital he made at Ravenna, which bears even to-day the marks of his residence, especially in its marvelous mosaics; but he loved Pavia and Verona also, though there no monuments of him remain.

In the year 500, he visited Rome. He came as a Christian, and not as an Arian, for he went first to Saint Peter's and prayed at the Apostle's grave, "with great piety, and as if he were a Catholic," a chronicler remarks. Then he went over the Ponte S. Angelo, and so into the city. This became the stereotyped route for emperors entering Rome; it was followed three hundred years later by Charlemagne.

In Rome, Theodoric lodged on the Palatine. The Senate met, and he addressed them, though his pronunciation was doubtless poor. In the Latin of the address, however, he may well have been assisted by his able secretary, Cassiodorus, of whom we shall have something to say later. It is a curious combination, Cassiodorus, the Last of the Senators, and Theodoric, the First of the Gothic kings.

During this Roman visit he arranged that two hundred pounds weight of gold (somewhat over two hundred thousand francs) should be spent every year for the restoration of the Palatine. He was also interested in the draining of the Pontine Marshes, and in the restoration of the Appian Way, and a memorial, even if a mistaken one, of his residence in the Campagna, is the name Palazzo di Teodorico, which is given to the ruins on the cliff above Terracina. Thus he verified what the brick stamps say of him, "Theodoric born for the good of Rome."

His feelings toward Rome are given us in an edict (Cass. *Var.* VII, 15), in words which might well be taken to heart by modern Rome: "The glorious buildings of Rome ought to have an expert guardian, that this wonderful forest of walls may be preserved with proper diligence, and the modern appearance of the work may be conserved with suitable dispositions." . . . Continuing, he speaks of the seven wonders of the world, and adds: "But who will think longer of them, when he has beheld so many amazing things in one single city. We give credit to these seven wonders because they belong to an older age, and whatever new thing was done in primitive times has always been rightly considered as excellent. But now it can only be called the truth, if Rome be said to be a miracle."

Still more remarkable is a passage in which he speaks of the aqueducts, those same aqueducts, which his successor, another Gothic king, but of a different stamp, was so ruthlessly to cut in the struggle for the capture of Rome. The passage in question was of course written by Cassiodorus, but in the name of the Emperor and with his approval (Cass. *Var.* VII, 6): —

One of the extraordinary things about the City of Rome is the remarkable healthfulness of the water, for these streams are brought here, as it were, by the building of mountains. From the solidity of the rock you might well think they were natural channels, because they are able to restrain so strongly for so many centuries such a force of flowing waters. Mountains themselves often cave in and disappear, and the channels of torrents are changed, but this work of the men of old time is not destroyed, provided it be protected with proper diligence. Consider what an ornament to Rome this mass of water provides! For in what would the beauties of the baths consist if they did not have these sweet waters? There runs the Aqua Virgo, so delightful and pure, and doubtless it received its name for this very reason, because it is defiled by no impurities. . . . The Aqua Claudia by a vast construction rises to the top of the Aventine, and when it comes tumbling down from the top, it seems to water alike the tip of the summit and the depths of the valley. . . . The Aqua Claudia in Rome, crossing the dry summits of so many mountains, gives forth from its bosom streams of pure water for washing-pools and for houses, and flows so equally that it never fails when it is wanted.

The man who had a love of these things saw the vision of a Gothic kingdom in Italy, which should bring to Rome the new blood which she needed, and should take and respect those treasures of the past with which Italy was still so well supplied. But not only did his ideal fail of fulfillment for lack of a capable successor; but by the closing acts of his life doubt springs up within us as to whether even the best Gothic spirit was capable of holding continuously to this lofty ideal. In almost the last year of Theodoric's reign his religious tolerance gave way under the strain of seeing Catholics in the East persecuting the Arians; and on the charge of conspiracy, Symmachus and Boethius were put to death after a most unjust trial. It was an unfortunate method of reverencing CIVILITAS, which led Theodoric to put to death two of the finest representatives of ancient Rome. They gave their lives for a philosophical concept, the liberty of Rome, as incorporated in the Senate of Rome. The next year (August 30, 526), Theodoric himself died and was buried in his own mausoleum at Ravenna.

His ten-year-old grandson, Amalasuntha's boy, Athalaric, ascended the throne, and for lack of a worthy successor Theodoric's dream of a great Gothic kingdom in Italy was straightway cheated of its fulfillment. For only a quarter of a century more the Gothic kingdom was to struggle along after a certain fashion, and then the Goths themselves were to leave Italy, and the place thereof was to know them no more.

And so we pass to the second half of our story of the Goths, the account of how Justinian restored Italy to the Eastern Empire. In the year 527, Justinian became Emperor at Constantinople. It is in the main his generals, Belisarius and Narses, who command our respect, and not the Emperor himself, but we cannot forbear a word about his character. He is the extreme type of a great legislator and a poor executive officer, — one of those men, who know mankind in theory, but not in practice, who have the skill to legislate for a nation, but are unable to set their own house in order, who are careful to bridle luxury and excess, but marry women of low and extravagant tastes. Justinian, as the successor of Gaius, and the ancestor of Blackstone, merits our profound admiration; Justinian, as the consort of the menagerie-keeper's daughter, Theodora, is a pitiful spectacle.

If, however, as is sometimes asserted, greatness consists in the ability to find efficient and faithful subordinates, Justinian deserves the title of great, because of his two generals, Belisarius and Narses. Our story concerns itself first with Belisarius.

In the year 526, when Belisarius was twenty-one years old, he was given the command of Justinian's Persian expedition, and within seven years he obtained the "Endless Peace" between the Empire and Persia. But Justinian's great ambition was to destroy the Vandal Kingdom, and restore North Africa to the Empire. Thither, then, Belisarius was sent, and within the year his work was completed. It was a fateful work, and pregnant with far-reaching consequence, for the destruction of the Vandal Kingdom removed from North Africa the one great obstacle in the way of the Moorish invasion which was to follow a century later, and if Belisarius had never lived, there might never have been the Battle of Tours.

Meantime affairs in Italy had been going badly. The young king, Athalaric, was being brought up in a most unfortunate manner by his mother, Amalasuntha. His education, or rather the ill-advisedness of it, caused his death in 534, after a nominal reign of but eight years. The queen mother, left alone, promptly associated with herself a Gothic noble, by name Theodahad. The relation was merely official, not personal, for her partner was already married. Within a few months, however, Theodahad had accomplished the death of Amalasuntha at the lonely lake of Bolsena, and was reigning alone.

Theodahad's bad behavior was Justinian's opportunity to effect the conquest of Italy, and thither the tireless Belisarius was sent. The actual warfare is preceded by a strange exhibition of diplomacy, when Theodahad offers to sell his crown to Justinian, and the following correspondence passes. I quote the two letters in Hodgkin's spirited translation (*Italy and Her Invaders*, vol. IV, p. 15 ff.).

Theodahad to Justinian: —

I am not, O Emperor, a newcomer into the halls of kings. It was my fortune to be born a king's nephew and to be reared in a manner worthy of my race: but I am not altogether well versed in war and its confusions. From the first I have been passionately fond of literature, and have spent my time in the study thereof, and thus it has been till now my lot to be always far from the clash of arms. It seems, therefore, unwise of me to continue to lead a life full of danger for the sake of the royal dignity, when neither danger nor dignity is a thing that I enjoy. Not danger, since that new and strange sensation perturbs my thoughts; not the royal dignity, since possession of it has, according to the general law, brought satiety. Therefore, if some landed property could be secured to me, bringing in a yearly income of not less than twelve hundred weight of gold [about a million and a quarter francs], I should consider that more valuable to me than my kingship; and I am willing on these terms to hand over to thee the sovereignty of the Goths and Italians. I think that I shall thus be happier as a peaceful tiller of the soil than as a king immersed in kingly cares, no sooner out of one danger than into another. Send me, then, as speedily as possible a commissioner to whom I may hand over Italy and all that pertains to my kingship.

The following is Justinian's reply: —

I heard long ago by common fame that you were a man of high intelligence, and now I find by experience that this is true. You show your wisdom in declining to await the arbitrament of war, which has plunged some men, who staked their all upon it, into terrible disasters. You will never have occasion to repent having turned us from an enemy into a friend. You shall receive all the property that you ask for, and, in addition, your name shall be inscribed in the highest rank of Roman nobility. I now send Athanasius and Peter to exchange the needful ratifications, and in a short time Belisarius will come to complete the transaction thus settled between us.

Meantime, Belisarius was pressing on. He passed rapidly from Carthage to Syracuse, thence to Palermo and Messina, and so to the mainland at Reggio. Thence he advanced on Naples and began the siege. In spite of brave resistance, the city was finally captured by the expedient of using the aqueducts as means of approach. Naples having been captured, Belisarius marched on Rome.

The fall of Naples convinced the Goths of the uselessness of their king, Theodahad, who, in spite of the diplomatic negotiations with Justinian, had not as yet resigned. Accordingly they held a great council on the Pontine Marshes, on a plain not far from Terracina, deposed Theodahad, and chose Witigis as their king. The first act of Witigis was to kill Theodahad; the second was to abandon Rome, leaving a mere perfunctory garrison, and to retreat to Ravenna.

When Belisarius, therefore, arrived from Naples, coming along the Via Latina, he marched in by the Porta Asinaria, while the Gothic garrison abandoned the city by the Porta Flaminia. This error on the part of Witigis is an interesting example of the practical value of ideals. Had Witigis been more of an idealist, had he appreciated more truly the sentimental value of Rome, he would not have made the tactical error of abandoning the city. It was true then, as it has been true ever since, that he who holds Rome holds Italy. He soon realized his mistake, but it was too late, and thus the long siege of Rome began. It was the month of December, 536, when the troops of Belisarius marched into Rome. It was not, however, until the following March that the siege began. During these intervening three months, Belisarius made his preparations. Outside of the city he captured Narni, Spoleto, and Perugia. In the city itself he repaired the old walls of Aurelian, which had been last restored by Honorius a century and a quarter before.

Meantime the Gothic king, Witigis, had raised at Ravenna an army which is said to have contained one hundred and fifty thousand men, and with this force he now marched southwards, and surrounded the city by seven Gothic camps. The siege, the most memorable that Rome ever suffered, lasted three hundred and seventy-four days. It is full of picturesque incidents, into which we have no time to enter, among them the attack on Hadrian's Mausoleum, which was defended at the cost of hurling the statues down on the Goths. But the most memorable event was the cutting of the aqueducts by the Goths. The consequences of this action were twofold. The immediate result was that, while the

Goths could cut the aqueducts, they could not stay their flow, and the continual outpouring of them changed the Campagna near Rome into a morass, with the consequent increase of malaria, so that the Goths were decimated and compelled to abandon the siege. Thus the aqueducts gave their life for the salvation of Rome. There was, however, another and much more diastrous result, in that, by the destruction of these aqueducts, the custom of bathing was discontinued. To be sure, the baths were disapproved of by the church, because of their immorality, but had the aqueducts and the baths continued, they would have been purified in time by the church and doubtless finally accepted. Thus the sanction of Christian Rome would have been placed on the habit of bathing, and obedience to Rome and imitation of her would have made the custom universal in the Western world. It is safe to say that, had the Goths not cut the aqueducts, bathing would have been as customary in Europe as it is in Japan. There would have been no need of the renaissance of bathing which the nineteenth century brought.

Within two years Italy was conquered by the Imperial troops, and Witigis was carried to Constantinople where he died in 540. However, the Gothic cause in Italy gradually regained its strength, and in 541 it obtained a splendid leader in the person of the newly appointed king Totila. Four years later, in the autumn of 545, Totila began the second Gothic siege of Rome. On

December 17, 546, the Porta Asinaria was treacherously
opened to the Goths, and Rome was again captured and
sacked. The Roman garrison escaped by the Porta
Flaminia, and there were left only a few hundred inhabitants. Then Totila formed the infamous plan of
destroying Rome, so entirely had the CIVILITAS of
Theodoric been forgotten. But Belisarius remonstrated
with him in a very wonderful letter, which Procopius
(*B. G.* III, 22) has preserved to us. Once again I use
Hodgkin's translation, for, though it is slightly free, especially toward the end, it gives a splendid impression of
the spirit of the letter: —

Fair cities are the glory of the great men who have been
their founders, and surely no wise man would wish to be remembered as the destroyer of any of them. But of all cities
under the sun, Rome is confessed to be the greatest and most
glorious. No one man, no single century, reared her greatness.
A long line of kings and emperors, the united efforts of some of
the noblest of men, a vast interval of time, a lavish expendi-
ture of wealth, the most costly materials, and the most skillful
craftsmen of the world have all united to make Rome. Slowly
and gradually has each succeeding age there reared its monuments. Any act, therefore, of wanton outrage against this
city will be resented as an injustice by the men of all ages, by
those who have gone before us, because it effaces the memorials
of their greatness, by those who shall come after, since the
most wonderful sight in the world will no longer be theirs to
look upon. Remember, too, that this war must end either in
the Emperor's victory or your own. If you should prove to be
the conqueror, how great will be your delight in having preserved the most precious jewel in your crown. If yours should
turn out to be the losing side, great will be the thanks due from

the conquerors for the preservation of Rome, while its destruction would make every plea for mercy and humanity on your part inadmissible. And, last of all, comes the question, what shall be your eternal record in history, whether you will be remembered as the preserver or the destroyer of the greatest city of the world?

The city was spared, but Totila abandoned it immediately with his army, and for forty days Rome was uninhabited. These forty days are the only break in a sequence of three thousand years of human habitation on this spot.

At the end of forty days, or thereabouts, Belisarius by a clever cavalry movement recaptured the city, and the Imperial troops remained in possession until 549, when the city fell once again into the hands of Totila. On this occasion Totila showed himself such an entire convert to the ideal of Belisarius that now it was not a question of destroying but rather of rebuilding Rome; and once more races were held in the Circus Maximus. But this restoration of Gothic CIVILITAS was shortlived. Justinian's second general, the eunuch, Narses, was sent to Italy, and with his coming, and the "Battle of the Apennines" (552), Totila was defeated and killed. In the next year the Goths moved out of Italy and were lost to history.

It was less than seventy years since Theodoric had led his nation across the Alps. During these years the great Gothic kingdom in Italy had been established; and it was only twenty-seven years since its founder had

died. But twenty-seven years, at the hands of Belisarius and Narses, sufficed to destroy this kingdom, and
with its destruction to render hopeless the ideal of preserving Roman culture. Theodoric's solution had failed;
and we must now turn to Benedict.

To understand, however, what Benedict did, we must
first consider for a moment the history of Christianity
since Constantine. In the last two centuries of the Roman Republic we saw the rise of individualism, in connection with the pathological growth of extreme self-
consciousness, which arose under conditions of self-indulgence. We saw this instinct manifesting itself along
religious lines in a morbid concern for personal salvation. We saw the attempted solutions of this religious
need, first in philosophy, and then in the cults of the
Orient. Among these latter cults it was Christianity
which offered the most interesting solution, for while it
recognized the individualistic tendency, it also strove to
correct it by its accentuation of man's responsibilities to
those about him. One of its fundamental doctrines was
the bearing of one another's burdens; and those who had
ears to hear might realize the hard saying that he that
loseth his soul shall find it, and he that findeth his soul
shall lose it. But these lofty ideals were not carried out
in practice, and a great many adherents of the new religion were primarily concerned with the cultivation and
salvation of their individual souls. There was also the
Oriental element in Christianity, common to it and all

the other religions of the Orient, which caused it to despise this present world, and to focus its attention on the life to come. Its lessons of helpfulness and philanthropy were entirely forgotten in the presence of the pressing need of securing one's own salvation. But this contempt of the present life was not confined to a contempt of the world itself; it included also the individuals in the world. The Christians felt themselves to be elect above their fellows and took supreme satisfaction in this realization. But as the Christian community grew in numbers, so their feeling of superiority was more insufficiently satisfied. Beyond all this, it was doubtless true that, when the masses accepted Christianity, its ideals inevitably suffered, and its demands were lowered. In 340, a church council declared that the Gospel injunctions about poverty were not intended for the ordinary Christian. Thus, unconsciously, a double standard was established, that of the ordinary and of the extraordinary Christian; and those men, of whom there are always a certain number in every community, who desired a more perfect way, could find this more perfect way only by leaving the world, and retreating into solitude, where their own higher ideals would be uninterrupted. In this way only could they obtain that feeling of especial electness above their fellows. And thus out of the Ascetic grew the Anchorite, the Hermit.

There was, however, another and a nobler reason which attracted men to the solitary life. During these centuries men of individuality and ability had few chances to lead an active life, a life with a purpose. The cultivation of religion, however, offered such activity. The life of voluntary renunciation gave more fully even of this present life, than could the acceptance of the status of placid nonentity.

Thus in the great economy of nature, with the breakdown of the outer world, there went the building-up of the inner world, — "the kingdom of Heaven is within you." On this principle men lost the world in order that they might find it; and as the inner life grew in reality, the outer life became more and more unreal. We can trace the growth of this movement as early as the end of the second century, when Tertullian declaims against it, asserting that Christians are not SILVICOLÆ or EXULES VITÆ. But nevertheless the Solitaries continued to increase. It was Upper Egypt, especially the region near Thebes, which was favored by these Solitaries. There the Hermit Paul (228–341) went into the desert at twenty-three, and lived in solitude for ninety years; and there Antony (251–356) passed the best part of a century. But women as well as men sought the better way; for example, the penitents, Thais and Pelagia.

But human nature enjoys receiving credit for its virtue, and a man in the desert would be of necessity deprived of an audience. Thus altitude was substituted for latitude and the Stylitæ arose, men who lived on the tops of pillars, with their prototype, Simon Stylites of

Antioch. Even more grotesque and terrible were those who walled themselves up from the waist down, like a certain enthusiast near Tours.

But man is by nature a sociable animal, and the hermit is the exception. Accordingly, when the craze for Anchoritism had subsided, those who still desired to leave this evil world evolved the idea of leaving it in companies. They would thus be able to combine solitude and companionship. Thus began monastic life. It is significant that it, too, began in Egypt, where Pachomius, about the middle of the fourth century, ruled over fourteen hundred brethren, divided into nine communities. The importance of Pachomius is only just beginning to be realized. Born about 285, he began life as a monk of Serapis, and his biographer tells us that he employed his time in raising vegetables and palms for his own use and for the benefit of his neighbors. Being converted to Christianity, he joined a colony of hermits, a sort of intermediate stage between the solitary hermit and the fully organized monastery. It seems to have been at this time that he recognized the advantages of companionship, and conceived the idea of an organized monastic life. What makes his case especially interesting is his early connection with Serapis; for while the Christian monasticism of Egypt is not derived from Serapis, it is possible that Serapis may have influenced it in some minor points, as, for example, in the tonsure. Slightly later, the Hungarian Martin founded a monastery, first at Milan, and later at Tours. Thus in the Western Empire, and somewhat similarly in the Eastern Empire, Monastic communities were springing up. It is important to realize that these monks were laymen, and proud of their position. In fact, at this time the monks were in dread of being ordained. But there were two dangers to which these monasteries were exposed: there was, on the one hand, the danger that they might grow lawless and uncontrolled, and their inmates therefore idlers and vagabonds; and there was also the danger that they might fall entirely under the domination of the priests.

Because it satisfied a real human need, the institution of monasticism was destined to grow greater with succeeding centuries, but if it were to be of any profit to the world at large, it must be controlled and put to work. This was the task of Benedict, and if one wishes to estimate the value of his accomplishment, one has but to look at the Eastern Empire, where there was a Basil but no Benedict, i.e., no principle of stability and useful occupation.

Benedict was born about 480, at Norcia, the ancient Nursia, the *frigida Nursia* of Virgil's *Æneid*, a small town about twenty miles east of Spoleto. In sharp contrast to Augustine, we know nothing of his mother. His father, Euprobus, was a Roman of noble birth. For the facts of Benedict's life we are largely dependent on the *Vita*, written by his disciple, Pope Gregory the Great; for the spirit and personality of the man we may go to

Benedict's *Rule.* The former source of information, Gregory's *Vita*, is disappointing. It deals largely with the miracles of Benedict, a theme in which Gregory was especially interested, and gives relatively little insight into his character; the latter of our sources, the *Rule*, is admirable so far as it goes; and a careful study of it brings us much nearer to a knowledge of the man than would at first sight seem possible.

When at a tender age and while still under the tutelage of a pedagogue, Benedict came to Rome, and to his father's house, which is supposed to have been in Trastevere on the site of the modern Church of S. Benedetto, in Piscinula. But if we are correctly informed, his stay in Rome was short, and his sensitive youth was so terrified by the wickedness of the city that he straightway went into the desert. For him this desert was not Egypt, but the upper valley of the Anio. It is significant of the devastation wrought by the wars and rumors of war, that this region, where once had stood Horace's Sabine farm, with its atmosphere redolent of peace, and Nero's villa, with its gardens and chain of artificial lakes, should be at this time a wilderness.

The story of Benedict's wandering is a series of beautiful pictures, which may easily be called legends, but may equally well, for the major part at least, represent historical facts. There is no profit in approaching these stories in a rationalistic spirit. If we are to enter at all into sympathy with Benedict's life, and into the atmosphere of his age, we must accept these stories without dispute and enjoy their beauty. At Subiaco, forty-four miles from Rome, Benedict met a certain Romanus, who showed him a cave in which Benedict dwelt alone for three years. His food was lowered to him from the top of the cliff in a basket, and a terra-cotta bell, such as is still so common in the Abruzzi, tied at the end of a rope, called him from his devotions to partake of his meals. But one day the Devil, observing his method of life, broke the bell by throwing a stone at it, and Benedict was in danger of starvation. But a good presbyter was warned of the Lord in a vision, and he took his Easter fare with him in a basket and sought the cave and found Benedict. It was in these years that when tempted by the lust of the flesh, he threw himself into a thicket of thorns to conquer the temptation. This thicket still grows by the mouth of the cave, but it is a rosebush now ever since the visit of the gentle Saint Francis. It is of these years that Benedict is thinking in the first part of his *Rule*, when he speaks of the life of the Anchorites.

The second class of monks is that of the Anchorites, that is to say, of the Hermits. These men, not under the influence of conversion, and with the fervor of the novice, but having had first a long experience in a monastery, and having been taught by the aid of many, have learned how to fight the Devil, and thus, being well instructed by fighting shoulder to shoulder with their brothers, they are able at last, with the aid of God, to fight in safety, without the help of others, but by their own hand and their own arm alone, against the sins of the flesh and evil thoughts.

Between the lines we can read the recollection full of pity for the young boy who suffered alone in the thicket of thorns.

At this time the monks of Vicovaro desired to have Benedict as their abbot. It was in one of their reactionary moments, when they confused temporary satiety with true repentance. When they came to their truer and worse selves again, they rebelled against him. It is interesting that he, who, as the father of all Western monks, was to rule for centuries after his death, was unable to control this, his first monastery. Finally they tried to poison him, but he escaped by a miracle and returned to the wilderness. He was learning by experience the necessity of a "rule" for monks. Later he established twelve monasteries in the valley of Subiaco, and was joined by his faithful disciples, Maurus and Placidus. But the strife of the communities was so great that he left Subiaco in 528, and proceeded across the mountains until he came to the site of an old temple of Apollo on Monte Cassino, where he founded his monastery.

At Monte Cassino he abode for fifteen years, until his death in 543. It was there that he passed those years which were so troublous for Italy and which we described at the beginning of the chapter, the turmoil of Amalasuntha, Theodahad, Witigis, and Totila. There from the peace of the mountain-top he could look down on the long stretch of the Via Latina and see the troops marching north and south, now Belisarius, now the

Ostrogoths. But except for one visit from Totila, he seems to have lived apart from it all.

Turning now from Benedict to his *Rule,* we may notice that in comparison with the extremes to which monastic discipline was usually carried it was to be an easy rule. The beautiful prologue begins thus: —

Hear, O my son, the teachings of the master, and incline the ear of thy heart, and receive with joy the command of a loving father, and fulfill it industriously, in order that, by the labor of obedience, thou mayest return unto him from whom by the slothfulness of disobedience thou hadst departed. For to thee now my words are directed, whosoever thou art, who givest up thine own sinful desires, and art ready to fight for the Lord Christ, the true king, and to take the strong and noble arms of obedience. . . . We are to establish, therefore, a school for the service of the Lord; and in this institution we hope that we are not about to prescribe anything which is harsh or burdensome. But if, obeying the dictates of reason and of justice, and for the sake of correcting human faults and preserving charity, we may seem in some things to have been a trifle too strict, do not take fright and flee away from the path of salvation. For the way of salvation must needs have a narrow beginning, but in the progress of spiritual life and of faith, and as our heart grows wider, it is with an indescribable sweetness of love that we run in the way of the commandments of the Lord. Therefore, never departing from his teaching, and living our life in his doctrines in the monastery even unto death, let us in patience share in the Passion of Christ, that we may be worthy to be with Him in his kingdom.

One of the prime requirements is the principle of STABILITAS. Vagabondage and the bands of itinerant monks are strictly forbidden: "The fourth class of monks

are those who are called 'Wanderers,' who throughout
their whole life in various provinces abide for three or four
days at a time in various cells, always wandering, and
never abiding, given over to their own desires and the
lusts of the flesh." But if monks are to be content to
live their lives in one place, they must be kept occupied;
hence the spirit of work which breathes out of the *Rule*.
We see this, for example, in section 48, "Concerning the
Daily Work of the Hands": "Idleness is the enemy of
the soul. Therefore, at certain times the brothers
should occupy themselves with the labor of the hands,
and similarly at certain hours with the reading of the
Scriptures." Then follows a detailed disposition of the
hours of the day, according to the season of the year.
The rules for the observance of Lent are especially interesting: "In the days of Lent, moreover, from the morning until the end of the third hour, let them give their
attention to reading, and from then until the end of the
tenth hour, let them labor at that which has been given
them to do. In the days of Lent, let them all receive
from the library one book apiece and let each one read
his book through. These books are to be given at the
beginning of Lent. But above all, let there be appointed
one or two elders, that, during the hours when the
Brethren are occupied with reading, they may pass
through the Monastery to see if by any evil chance there
be found any brother who is idle or who is gossiping or
who is not busy with the reading. For such an one not

only does evil himself, but also disturbs the others. And if any such idle brother be found — may it not be so! — let him be rebuked for the first and the second time; and if he does not mend his ways, let him be subjected to a regular punishment, such that the rest may fear."

Benedict's motto was "Pax," and no one can read the *Rule* without a great desire to seek peace and pursue it. The ends to be obtained are goodness and discipline and knowledge. There is a deep reverence in the whole book, as, for example, in the twentieth section, "Concerning the Reverence of Prayer": "If when we wish to obtain a favor from powerful men, we do not presume to ask it except with humility and reverence, how much more should we pray with all humility and pure devotion to the Lord God of all. For we know that we are not heard for our much speaking, but according to the purity of our heart and the genuineness of our tears. Thus our prayer should be short and simple, unless perchance, by the inspiration of the Divine Grace, it be prolonged. But when prayer is made in common, it should be short, and at a sign from the Superior all should rise together."

There is also abundance of hospitality, as many scholars still experience to-day at Monte Cassino. This is laid down in two marvelous paragraphs (53): —

Let all strangers who come be received as though they were Christ, because one day He will say to you, "I was a stranger, and ye took me in." And let honor be shown to them all, but especially to the servants of the faith and to pilgrims. And as soon as a stranger is announced, let him be met by the Prior or by the Brethren with every loving attention. And let them first pray together, and then let them be united in the kiss of peace. But let not the kiss of peace be given, until prayer has first been made, on account of the machinations of the Devil. And in the salutation of those who come or of those who go, let great humility be shown, and with the body prostrate on the ground, let Christ be adored in them, even as He is received in them.

Then follow a series of minor rules thought out with loving care: that at the coming of strangers the abbot should break his fast, unless it be one of the major fasts, which must not be broken, but in any case the Brethren should continue fasting; that they should give them water for their hands, and wash their feet. But above all, especial care and attention should be shown to the poor, "because that in them most particularly Christ is received." "Let the bedroom for the strangers be under the care of a Brother whose soul is filled with the fear of God, and in this room let there be beds made ready in abundance, and let the house of God be governed wisely. And let no one to whom it is not commanded speak to these strangers, but if he meets them or sees them, let him salute them with humility, as has been said, and, asking their blessing, pass by them, explaining that he is not allowed to speak with them." The sixty-first chapter contains special rules for the entertainment of pilgrim monks: "If any pilgrim monk shall come from the far-away provinces, and shall wish to abide as a guest in the monastery, and if he shall be content with the habits of the place as he finds it, and shall not disturb the monastery by his presence, but shall show himself content, let him be received for as long a time as he desires. If, however, he finds fault or makes criticisms reasonably and with loving humility, let the Abbot give careful attention to his suggestions, for perhaps God may have sent the stranger there for that very purpose."

It is again this same humility which comes to expression in the beautiful words with which the *Rule* closes: "And thou, whoever thou art, who art hastening to the Heavenly country, fulfill first with the aid of Christ this little rule of introduction here laid down. So then, with the help of God, thou shalt come to the greater heights of doctrine and of virtue, of which we have spoken above. Amen! Explicit Regula."

In a moment we shall speak of the effects of the *Rule*, but first it was necessary that one complementary thing should be added. The organization was there, the requirement of mental labor was there, but the actual copying and preservation of manuscripts were not specified. These elements come into existence at the same time, but in two places very far apart in the Western world, at Scyllacæum, in southern Italy, and at Arles, in southern France. The monastery at Squillace (Scyllacæum) was founded by Cassiodorus the Senator, the Chancellor of Theodoric the Ostrogoth. Born about the same year as Benedict, he retired from active life about 540, when he was sixty years old, having spent forty years in the service of the Gothic Court. Feeling that in a certain sense his life had been wasted, he became a monk and retired to his beloved Calabria, where he turned his ancestral villa into a monastery, famous for its copying-room, and especially for its book-binding, where " the wedding garments" for books were made, and where he labored for thirty-three years, until his death. A similar copying-room was introduced by the Abbess Cæsaria at Arles at about this same time or somewhat earlier.

As for the success of Benedict's *Rule* it was not in rivalry to any existing rules, but only in completion of them. Hence it met with little or no opposition, and soon became so universal in Western Europe that the Council of Aix (862) proclaimed it the only rule.

Thus the Benedictines stepped forward into modern Europe. They carried not only the cross and the plow; they carried also the pen. They were not only the greatest missionaries, they were not only the greatest farmers, they were also the scholars and the schoolmasters. They carried Christianity, but they carried it in peaceful union with ancient culture. In England, Germany, Denmark, Sweden, Poland, Bohemia, they did the work of intellectual pioneers; and during the sixth, seventh, eighth and ninth centuries they not only converted Europe, but they also civilized her. Theirs was not simply the work of copying the classics; they were also the historians and librarians of Europe. Think only of York in the seventh century, and of Farfa in the eleventh. Think of the printing-press at Subiaco, and that at Westminster. Go back again to the tenth century, and see one of the world's great writers, Hrotswitha, the Benedictine abbess of Gandersheim (935–1001); and look in the eleventh century at the renewal of the world which came forth from the monastery of Clairvaux in France, and the abbey of Quedlinburg in Germany.

The Gothic Kingdom might fail, but the heritage of the past was not to be lost, and the little boy who had fled away from the wickedness of Rome, now grown to be a man, with his companions, on the site of the temple of Apollo, was to do Apollo's bidding as well as Christ's in keeping alive for the world that "sweetness and light" which was no enemy of Him, who came not to destroy but to build up.

CHAPTER VIII

GREGORY AND THE LOMBARDS: THE PREPARATION FOR
THE HOLY ROMAN EMPIRE

WE reach to-day our journey's end. It seems a very
short time since we stood at the beginning of that journey, at the other end of the path, and beheld it stretching
before us. We were standing then in the midst of a very
primitive people, devoid entirely of what we call culture in the larger sense. They were so crude and their
faces were so entirely turned to the ground, their consciousness was so saturated with purely physical needs,
that they had not as yet acquired even a rudimentary
sense of patriotism. We have followed these people
through the great educational processes which history
brought them. We saw them nursed into the religion of
patriotism by the Etruscans; we saw them tutored into
the religion of beauty by the Greeks. We admired their
power of adaptation in entertaining these foreign ideas,
but we saw also the disadvantages which are inevitably
connected with such foreign importations. Their simple
and practical scheme of religion became entangled by
the luxurious overgrowth of superstition, and all that
was necessary to turn their over-faith into under-faith
— that is, scepticism — was an excess of material prosperity. The Punic Wars brought this prosperity and the
decline of faith followed.

But while prosperity caused faith to decline, it aroused men to a sense of individuality. Thus individualism in other things and also in religion came into the life of Rome. To meet this new religious need, there were present two sources of supply: on the one hand, philosophy; on the other, the cults of the Orient. We watched the struggle of these rival ideas, and saw the victory of Christianity. But after this preliminary conquest, a more intense struggle took place, the struggle between the ancient culture and the new religion. Then Rome began to be divided against herself; Constantinople was born and assumed the dignity of the capital. The East became separated from the West. In the West itself, Milan and Ravenna began to surpass Rome. And all the while beneath these divisions there were still other divisions. There was the great schism between the old ideas and the new; between the old instincts of patriotism and social solidarity and the new ideas, which, whatever they may have been in theory, were in practice extraordinarily self-centred and anti-social. There was an organized government and a system of laws which, all of it, harked back to paganism, and there was a new religion whose most earnest devotees were interested principally in the saving of their own souls and the flight from the temptations of this present evil world.

And lastly, with the weakness of Rome, her borders ceased to be defended, and the Teutonic tribes, which had long been pressing against her gates, broke through and overran Italy. Thus the Visigoth and the Vandal robbed and pillaged Rome, while those who might have been her citizens and her defenders were saving their own souls in the desert and the cloister. Yet so great was the love that ancient culture called forth, and so resistant was she in her struggle for life, that these apparently tender things, these methods of thought, these legal ideas, these literary expressions, were able, at least in great part, to survive this turmoil. They kept their hold on the minds of at least the intellectual fathers of the church, they won the respect of the Ostrogoths, and they gained access even to the monasteries, where man had gone to escape the world. In our last lecture we have seen how, granted the inevitableness of monasticism, Benedict's *Rule* saved the day for ancient literature.

But in our gratitude for the existence of this great salvation, we overlooked the hard fact, that, though the monastery could secure the actual physical preservation of literature, and though its teachings might keep alive a love of the spirit as well as the letter, so that the copyist's heart would follow his pen, nevertheless the laws and institutions of the Roman Empire could not be compressed within the limits of a cloister. Greek art and Greek literature have been preserved, but Greece in its atmosphere and in its institutions has been lost. Thus Rome might have been preserved in her literature, and her law books might have been copied to infinity, but the living impress of Rome would have been lost. Only an established state could inherit the tradition of a state; it could live in a government with temporal power; it would die under the cloistered rule of a monastery.

There is, therefore, one chapter still left in our story. In it we are to study the rise of this temporal power, which was to carry on the form of Rome which the monastery could not contain; while the monastery was to preserve the spirit which this temporal power might or might not preserve. The rise of this power is one of the most wonderful things in the world's history; in a sense we can scarcely hope to understand it, but we can come near to an understanding by studying the outward phenomena, which are quite clear. To do this, however, we must go afield, far to the north, and study the rise and history of the Lombards.

The Lombards, or Langobardi, whose original name seems to have been the Winili, were settled originally in Scandinavia. Later they moved to the mouth of the Elbe, where their presence is attested by the geographical name Bardengau, obviously an abbreviation for Langobardengau. We hear of them, in A.D. 165, as crossing the Danube, and being defeated by the Romans and then for three hundred and fifty years they pass entirely out of history, until the time of Anastasius (491–518).

In the reign of their king, Audoin, Justinian made an

alliance with them, and they were permitted to settle in Noricum. But our real interest in them begins with Audoin's son, Alboin, for it was under his leadership that on April 2, 568, they began their invasion of Italy. According to tradition they came by invitation of Justinian's general, Narses. But too much weight should not be attached to such stories of invitations. The Lombards seem to have crossed the Alps by way of Villach and the Predil Pass, and thus they overran Venetia, and conquered Vicenza and Verona without difficulty. They then did a thing which none of their predecessors had done, and which was an omen of the fact that they had come to abide in Italy, and not to march away of their own will as the Visigoths had, or to be driven away as were the Ostrogoths. They shut, as it were, the door behind them. This they accomplished by establishing the duchy of Forum Julii, with Gisulf, the king's nephew as first duke, equipping him with a picked body of followers. Within the next three years, Milan and Pavia had both surrendered; and then, suddenly, at the height of his power, Alboin was brutally murdered (572).

After two years of confusion, the Lombards abandoned the idea of having a king; and Italy was ruled by an oligarchy of the "Thirty-six Lombard Dukes." This arrangement lasted for ten years. Thus were established in Italy thirty-six allied duchies, out of which in the course of time the city-states of the Middle Ages and of the Renaissance were to arise. So deep were these divisions to be impressed on the popular mind, and so strong was the instinct of the city-state to become, that even to-day, in the presence of the miracle of United Italy men are first of all Milanese or Siennese, and only secondly Italians, and their "country," their real "paese," is the old city-state.

Thus the Lombards were accomplishing already a great work of differentiation. By their system of duchies they were laying the foundations for the rise of the little city-states, which were to give an object for the exercise of that patriotism, which with the best will in the world could no longer cling to the ghost of the Roman Empire. Then, too, in this division of Italy was to lie its strength, and the distribution of responsible tasks among relatively few men was to produce the many-sided genius of the Renaissance.

But the Lombard Oligarchy was not only laying the foundations of this distant Italy; it was also preparing the way for the rise of the new Roman Empire, and it was doing this quite unconsciously by the invasion of Gaul, and the harassing of the Franks. For when in the course of time the Franks came to save the Pope from the hands of the unspeakable Lombards, they came, not simply because they were the "most Christian Franks," and because they loved the Pope, but they came even more for hatred of the Lombards. Thus the Lombards by their present invasions were raising against themselves a hatred which was in the course of time to be turned to the profit of the Papacy.

The rule of the Oligarchy came to an end in 584, when the Lombards chose Flavius Authari, the son of Cleph, to be their king. In the sixth year of his reign, Authari married Theudelinda, the daughter of Garibaldi, the Duke of the Bavarians. There is a promise of modern Italy in the father's name. In the following year (590) Authari died at Pavia.

His death brings Theudelinda into the centre of the picture, for the Lombards were so attached to her that they wished her to remain as queen, and promised that he to whom she should give her hand should be the king. She chose a certain Agilulf, the Duke of Turin (*dux Taurinatium*), and he was made king at Milan in 590, in the presence of all the Lombards. If we may trust the legend, Theudelinda solved in a charming way the difficulty of the position in which a queen is placed who must of necessity choose her own husband. She summoned to herself Agilulf and when he arrived, she met him as was the custom with the cup of welcome. As he took it from her hand, he touched her hand with his lips in sign of homage; but straightway she said to him, "Why should he kiss my hand, who has the right to kiss my lips?" Then the Duke knew that he had been chosen as her husband.

It was at Monza, near Milan, that Theudelinda caused a palace to be built, and its walls to be decorated with the deeds of the Lombards. "And in this painting," says Paul the Deacon, "it is clearly shown in what fashion the Lombards in those days trimmed the hair on their head, and of what fashion their clothing and their garments were. For they left the back of their neck bare, shaving it up to the top of the head, and they let their hair hang down in front as far as the mouth, parting it on the forehead. Their clothes were loose-cut and mostly of linen, such as the Saxons are accustomed to wear, and they had borders of various colors. Their boots were open to the end of the great toe, and held together by cross-lacing." We can see them clearly before our eyes, and in them we behold the Dante, and the Anselm, and the Lanfranc with which they were to endow Italy.

But this endowment was yet a long way off. Theudelinda was, however, preparing the way for it, and all because she happened to be Orthodox and not Arian. The single year of her married life with Authari did not suffice to enable her to influence his religion. But with Agilulf she was more successful, for, although he did not abandon the Arian faith of his fathers, he was on terms of friendship with the leaders of the Catholic faith, and even went so far as to permit Theudelinda to have her son baptized a Catholic. Agilulf reigned for twenty-five years (590–615), and it is during his reign that the figure of Gregory comes into prominence. To him we now turn.

The best source for Gregory's life is the collection of his own letters in twelve books, but we have also the life which Paul the Deacon wrote of him about 770, a life by John the Deacon a century later (872), a famous chapter in Bede's *Ecclesiastical History*, and certain passages in Gregory of Tours' *History of the Franks*.

The dates of Gregory's life until he was made pope, in 590, are very uncertain. He was born apparently about the year 540, of a noble Roman family. His father, Gordian, was a Regionarius, that is, a lay assistant to the deacon who had charge of one of the seven ecclesiastical regions into which the city of Rome had been divided. It was a position of political importance, and in this case its incumbent occupied a palace on the Cælian.

Gregory's family were involved in the religious fervor of the age, and in the tendency to flee from the world. No less than three of his aunts went into convents, but in one of them the love of the world was sufficiently strong to cause her to come out again and marry. This healthy love of the world seems also to have been characteristic of Gregory. He had a good education in Latin, but knew no Greek, and seems never to have learned it. This fact is impressive when we recollect that he was later six or seven years in Constantinople. It shows us how thoroughly Latin was still the language of the Court. We know very little of his childhood, but if it were spent in Rome, it must have been

a troubled one, for these are the years of Totila's repeated sieges and of the temporary abandonment of the
city.

Almost the first known event in his life dates from
about 573, when he was already thirty-three years of
age. In that year he held the office of Prefect of the city
of Rome. Although with the great decline of Rome, this
office must have been deprived of much of its significance, it is probable that it had not lost much of its
magnificence, though the symbols of that magnificence
might well have grown threadbare and shabby. The
Prefect of Rome was a very great personage. He was
President of the Senate, and went about clad in purple
and fine linen and wearing a sword. When he drove, it
was in a stately carriage drawn by four horses, decked
out with silver ornaments. He was in charge of all the
phases of the life of the city, from the control of the po-
lice to the distribution of the corn. We cannot, of course,
tell how much of these glories may have passed away
before Gregory's day. In any case he still held the civil
power entirely in his hands, while the *magister militum*
had the political and military power.

In the midst of these years of active and honorable
secular life, the call of the other-worldliness came to him,
and he became a monk, and, as Paul the Deacon says of
him, "He who had been accustomed before to walk
through the city clothed in the purple-bordered toga,
adorned with glittering jewels and wearing silken rai-

ment, was now a poor man ministering to the poor; and
clad in a wretched garment." We have no knowledge
in his case, as in that of Augustine, as to what inward
struggles had taken place in his soul. The passion for
the monastic life was very great at this time. Later,
when he had become pope, there were more than three
thousand nuns in the city of Rome itself who shared in
the patrimony of Saint Peter, and the number of monks
was of course very much larger still.

He threw himself entirely into this new life, and besides founding and endowing six Benedictine convents
in Sicily, he turned his father's house on the Clivus
Scaurus into a monastery and dedicated it to the Apostle
Andrew. This monastery was perhaps on the site of
the present Church of S. Gregorio. The number of
monks in Rome had increased greatly because of the
attacks which the Lombards were wont to make on
lonely monasteries, as, for example, on Monte Cassino,
which was attacked just about this time (577) and lay
in ruins for one hundred and forty years.

As for Gregory, having given away all that he had,
he became a monk in his own monastery. There he
allowed himself only the one luxury of a single piece of
plate, a silver dish, in which he ate the food which his
mother prepared for him. But one day a shipwrecked
sailor came to him and asked him for alms; he came
again, and again a third time; and Gregory, having
nothing else, gave him the silver dish.

It was at this time that those things happened to him of which Bede tells in the *Ecclesiastical History*. The story is old and familiar, and has sometimes been doubted, without sufficient reason; the word-plays in it are absolutely characteristic of Gregory and his age. I quote the incident in the quaint translation by Giles (*Hist. Eccl.* II, 1): —

It is reported that some merchants, having just arrived at Rome on a certain day, exposed many things for sale in the marketplace, and abundance of people resorted thither to buy: Gregory himself went with the rest, and among other things some boys were set for sale, their bodies white, their countenances beautiful, and their hair very fine. Having viewed them, he asked, as is said, from what country or nation were they brought, and was told from the island of Britain, whose inhabitants were of such personal appearance. He again inquired whether those islanders were Christians, or still involved in the errors of paganism, and was informed that they were pagans. Then, fetching a deep sigh from the bottom of his heart, "Alas, what pity," said he, "that the author of darkness is possessed of men of such fair countenances; and that, being remarkable for such graceful aspects, their minds should be void of inward grace." He therefore again asked, what was the name of that nation, and was answered that they were called Angles. "Right," said he, "for they have an angelic face, and it becomes such to be coheirs with the angels in heaven. What is the name," proceeded he, "of the province from which they are brought?" It was replied that the natives of that province were called Deiri. "Truly are they Deiri," said he, "withdrawn from wrath, and called to the mercy of Christ. How is the king of that province called?" They told him his name was Aella; and he, alluding to the name, said, "Hallelujah, the praise of God, the Creator, must be sung in those parts."

It was Gregory himself who started on this missionary journey. On the third day, while he and his companions were taking their noontide rest, a grasshopper lighted on the pages of the Bible, which Gregory was reading. "Ecce locusta," said he; "loco sta" (abide in this place), and thus he interpreted the omen to his companions; and shortly afterwards, before they had started again, messengers from Rome overtook them, bearing the commands of the Pope that Gregory should return. Thus ended his missionary journey. The story is probably true, and we have already seen Gregory's fondness for word-plays. This passion was the last estate of the long rhetorical training of the Empire.

When Gregory returned to Rome, the Pope appointed him "Seventh Deacon." We do not know exactly what the office of Seventh Deacon was, but it must have had some connection with the seven regions of Rome, each one of which was under the care of a deacon. The Seventh Deacon seems to have been the most important of all, and the position may have been regarded as leading to the Papacy. In 578, Pope Benedict (the First) died, and was succeeded by Pelagius the Second (578–90), that pope who restored the Church of S. Lorenzo, and whose name still stands on the triumphal arch. Pelagius seems to have recognized Gregory's ability, for he immediately appointed him to one of the two most important diplomatic positions in the church, sending him as Nuncio (*Apocrisiarius*) to Constantinople. At this time the Roman Church had two nuncios, one at Ravenna with the Exarch, and one at Constantinople with the Emperor. Of these the post at Constantinople was the more important. Gregory continued at Constantinople five or six years, and, while retaining his own interest in Rome as over against the East, and cherishing a contempt for Eastern methods and manners, he nevertheless succeeded in making friendships in the Imperial Court, especially with the Empress Constantina. These years in Constantinople were of great importance in Gregory's life, for it was then that he learned the entire indifference of the Eastern Empire to the affairs of Rome, and the hopeless incompatibility of the Eastern and the Western churches.

During these years the Empire was so occupied with its wars against the Persians that it had no time to attend to the affairs of Italy. In vain Pope Pelagius wrote to Gregory, urging him to make representations to the Emperor, that without his help "The Republic" could no longer be saved. This harking back of the phrase "The Republic" is almost ghastly in the reminiscences which it calls up, pictures of those long-ago days when the "Consuls were bidden to see to it that the Republic suffered no ill"; and now this Republic is beseeching an emperor at Constantinople, who has never seen Rome, to grant a *magister militum* and a *dux* for their protection. But these messages sent eastward proved of no avail, and so Pelagius shot an arrow westward at a venture. Turning to France, he wrote to the Bishop of Auxerre: "For we believe that for no other reason has it been ordained by Divine Providence, that your kings should hold the same orthodox confession of faith as the Roman Empire, save that they might be neighbors and helpers to this city, where this faith arose, and also to the whole of Italy."

These letters, coming as they do side by side, are of great importance, for they show that the diplomacy which afterwards resulted in the Holy Roman Empire did not grow up in the mind of any one man, but was a natural product of inevitable conditions.

About 585, Gregory returned to Rome, and became abbot of his own monastery of Saint Andrew. For the next five years we have no accurate knowledge of his life. They were dark and troubled years for the city of Rome. She was surrounded by the unspeakable Lombards, who were constantly pressing closer to her borders, and her territory was almost limited to that of the later Papal States. But war was not her only adversary; floods and pestilence were in her borders. Gregory of Tours gives us the account of an eye-witness, a deacon, whom he had sent to Rome, and who returned to him, relating that "in the ninth month of the last year (589) the river Tiber so overflowed its banks and covered the city of Rome that the ancient buildings fell in ruins, and even the granaries of the church, and many thousand bushels of grain were destroyed." He also told of a multitude of snakes and a great dragon which passed down the bed of the Tiber, and how the cattle were drowned by a tidal wave and thrown up on the shore. After the flood came the pestilence. This pestilence, coming up out of Egypt, had appeared at Constantinople a half century before. It caused a terror which can only be likened to that of the Black Death. In 590 it raged in Rome, as it had never raged there before, and threatened to destroy the entire population. In February the Pope Pelagius died of the plague, and the people insisted that Gregory should be his successor. But Gregory refused, and sent a letter to the Emperor Maurice to Constantinople, beseeching him to withhold his confirmation of the election; for without the approval of the Emperor the Bishop of Rome could not be consecrated. But this attempt on Gregory's part to escape the office was of no avail; for the Prefect of the city, learning of the matter, sent other letters urging the Emperor to confirm the election, and his messenger overtook the messenger of Gregory and substituted this letter for the one which Gregory had written.

Meantime, while they were awaiting the answer, Gregory was temporarily intrusted with the duties of pope. The chief concern of the city was the alarming ravages of the pestilence. On August 29, Gregory preached in the Church of Santa Sabina, on the Aventine, and his text was Jeremiah IV, 10: "The sword reacheth unto the soul." Amidst the ravages of the pestilence, and the oppression of the dog-days, — that peculiarly discouraging heat, which only a Roman summer day brings forth, — it is no wonder that his words were not forgotten by those who heard them, and that one of the audience, a certain deacon of Tours, remembered the discourse so well that when he returned home, he repeated it to his bishop, Gregory of Tours, in whose *History of the Franks* (x, 1) it has been preserved to us, as well as in Gregory's own works. I quote a passage from it, not only because it affords a good illustration of the power of Gregory's style, for he must have been a great orator; but also because it illustrates the continuance of the traditions of the classical school of rhetoric.

Dearly beloved Brethren, the judgments of God, which we have been taught that we ought to fear for the future, are now in our midst and fearfully to be dreaded; and may grief open up to us the way of repentance, and may the hardness of our hearts be softened by the sufferings which we endure. It was foretold of old by the prophet, "the sword has reached even unto the soul." For behold the whole people is smti en by the sword of the wrath of God, and one by one they are laid low by sudden death. Languor does not precede death, but, as you see, death itself anticipates lingering languor. For each one, struck down, is snatched away before he can turn to the lamentations of repentance. And what appearance would he make before his judge, the man who has had no chance to repent his deeds? It is not merely some of the inhabitants who are being taken away, but all alike are rushing to destruction. The houses are left empty, fathers behold the funerals of their sons, and one's heirs precede him to the grave. Let each one of us, therefore, take refuge in wailing and penitence, while there is still time to weep, ere we die. Let us recall before the eyes of our mind whatever errors we have committed, and let us repent in tears for our evil deeds. Let us come before Him in confession, and, as the prophet commands, let us raise our hearts with our hands unto the Lord. For he giveth courage for our prayer, He who cries through the mouth of his prophet, "I have no pleasure in the death of the wicked, but that the wicked turn from his way and live." Moreover, let none of us despair because of the magnitude of his evil deeds. For a three days' penitence purified even the men of Nineveh from their slothful sinfulness. And the thief that repented received the rewards of eternal life, even in the very article of death. Let us, therefore, experience a change of heart and believe that we have already received what we seek. . . . And since the sword of such great punishment is hanging over us, let us beseech him with importunate weeping, for that very importunity which is wont to be displeasing to men finds favor with the judge of truth. The pious and merciful God wishes us to pray to Him for pardon, for He is not willing to be angry with us according to our transgressions. Thus, He speaks through the mouth of the Psalmist: "Call upon me in the day of trouble, I will deliver thee, and thou shalt glorify me." He therefore is a witness unto Himself that He desires to have mercy upon those who call upon Him, because He admonishes us that He would be called upon. Therefore, dearest brethren, with contrite hearts and due repentance, and with the mind prepared for tears, come to the Sevenfold Litany on the fourth day of the week at dawn in the following order. Let all the regular clergy, therefore, together with the priests of the sixth region, start from the Church of the blessed martyrs, Cosmas and Damianus [in the Forum]. And let all the abbots, and under each abbot the monks of his monastery, together with the priests of the fourth region, set out from the Church, of the holy martyrs, Protasius and Gervasius [on the Quirinal]. Let all the abbesses, and under each abbess her nuns, together with the priests of the first region, start from the Church of the holy martyrs, Marcellinus and

Peter [Via Labicana, two miles out]. Let all the children, together with the priests of the second region, set out from the Church of the holy martyrs, John and Paul [on the Cælian]. Let all the laymen, together with the priests of the seventh region, start from the Church of the Holy First Martyr Stephen [near the Lateran]. Let all the widows, together with the priests of the fifth region, set out from the Church of Saint Euphemia [on the Viminal]. And let all the matrons, together with the priests of the third region, start from the Church of the holy martyr, Clement [near the Colosseum.] Proceeding from these various churches, let them gather together at the Basilica of the Blessed Mary, always a Virgin, Mother of our Lord Jesus Christ, that, there praying to God with prayer and wailing, we may prevail to merit pardon for our sins.

It takes no great effort of the imagination to see these seven choruses wending their way through the streets of Rome, and filling the air with their chants, each after its own fashion, as men, women, and children. And as we watch them slowly approaching Santa Maria Maggiore, we are reminded of those older Roman processions, especially that one of the year B.C. 207, when in the dread of the Second Punic War, three times nine maidens sang their choruses, and the procession of the people followed them up to the Aventine to the temple of Juno Regina. Then the material greatness of Rome was but beginning, and now it was long past. The glitter of gold and of marble had come and gone, and now there were ruins and broken columns. The physical greatness of Rome had come and gone; and amidst the ruins the strange idea of spiritual Rome was being

born, and lamentations and chants were her cradle-
song.

The procession itself afforded an additional proof of
the severity of the pestilence, for the same good deacon
of Tours, of whom we have already spoken, relates that
in one hour eighty of those who were taking part fell
dead to the ground. On the last day, the Friday (for
the penance had begun on the fourth day of the week,
Wednesday, and was to last three days), Gregory was
leading the chorus over the Bridge of Hadrian to worship at the tomb of Saint Peter. It was doubtless in the
late afternoon, as this prayer at Saint Peter's grave
would be a fitting close to the three days' ceremonies.
The sun may have been setting as they crossed the
bridge, and a golden glory would fill the sky behind the
Mausoleum of Hadrian. In that glory Gregory beheld
the angel Michael, with a flaming two-edged sword in
his hand; and as he looked, the archangel sheathed the
sword. Then Gregory knew that the pestilence was
ended; and thenceforth the Mausoleum of Hadrian was
called the Castle of S. Angelo.

This story has, of course, been doubted. It is not men-
tioned by Paul the Deacon, or by Bede, and occurs first
in the thirteenth century, but if it did not happen, it is a
pity it did not; and in any case it is too beautiful to pass
untold. Nor need we, with Gregorovius, suppose that a
broken piece of some ancient statue gave the impression
of an angel. Who would assert that Gregory did not see

an angel, especially if it happened at the sunset, when the heavens declare the glory of God, and the firmament showeth his handiwork?

Shortly after this, the confirmation of Gregory's election as pope arrived from Constantinople, and on September 3, 590, he was consecrated in Saint Peter's. The story of his attempts to escape, by causing himself to be smuggled out of Rome by merchants, is an invention of a later time, but we have one of his own letters in which he expresses his sorrow at the appointment. Historians have been at great pains to analyze his mental condition, with a view to ascertaining his sincerity, but all men of the greatness of Gregory have within them the element of contradiction, and they are entirely sincere in their apparent inconsistencies. It is a part of the price of genius that a man is never entirely happy in accepting or refusing any position in life.

Thus Gregory, at the age of fifty, began his life as pope, which was to last for fourteen years, and during which he was to lay the foundations of the Holy Roman Empire. If he had in any sense dreaded this life, because of its responsibilities and endless activities, the life itself proved the reasonableness of this dread.

It is impossible for us here to give more than a mere sketch of Gregory's occupations. They were the manifold works which would naturally fall to him who was the greatest man in the community, especially when that community was troubled without and within. It was not a question as to whether these were the things which a pope would ordinarily have done or not; they were obviously the things for Gregory to do, because they had to be done, and he was the only man who could do them. No one can accuse him of having sought power, the power was his, and he was compelled almost against his will to use it.

Let us consider first those things in his life which were the normal functions of the Pope. His most notable work here was the mission to England. He seems never to have forgotten his own interrupted journey, although it was not until the sixth year of his pontificate that he was able to send his substitute. In that year (596) he sent Augustine, the abbot of his own monastery of Saint Andrew. The story of this journey is intensely human. When Augustine and his companions arrived in Gaul, on their way to Britain, they were so terrified by the account of conditions in Britain, as described to them by the priests whom they met in Gaul, that they returned to Rome. But they were promptly sent back again by Gregory, and this time they went to their journey's end. Thus timidly did Augustine go forth to the immortal fame of being the first Bishop of Canterbury. The details of this mission do not concern us here, except that it is interesting to note that Gregory recognized the fact that the Christian Church already existed in Britain. There is a very beautiful letter of his to Augustine concerning this matter. The letter has been

preserved to us by Bede (*Hist. Eccl.*, I, 27), and I quote
it in Giles's translation. Augustine is asking a series of
questions which Gregory is answering: —

Augustine's second question: "Whereas the faith is one and
the same, why are there different customs in different churches
and why is one custom of masses observed in the Holy Roman
Church, and another in the Gallican Church."

Pope Gregory answers: "You know, my brother, the custom of the Roman Church in which you remember you were
bred up. But it pleases me that if you have found anything,
either in the Roman or the Gallican, or any other church,
which may be more acceptable to Almighty God, you carefully make choice of the same, and sedulously teach the Church
of the English, which as yet is new in the faith, whatsoever
you can gather from the several churches. For things are not
to be loved for the sake of places, but places for the sake of
good things. Choose, therefore, from every church those
things that are pious, religious, and upright, and when you
have, as it were, made them up into one body, let the minds of
the English be accustomed thereto."

These missionary cares were but a small segment of
Gregory's responsibilities. The routine of his daily life
was crowded with his duties as steward of the Patrimony
of Saint Peter's. We can scarcely realize to ourselves
the condition of Rome at this time. The atmosphere
was tense with the formal observance of religion. The
old pagan festivals had gone, except such of them as
lived on under the guise of Christian festivals. The idea
of the end of the world was still foremost in men's minds.
The tendency toward monastic life was so strong that
the Pope in Rome and the Emperor in Constantinople

both strove to repress it. For those who were not in the cloistered life, there was almost nothing left, except the army, by which they could fill their time and support themselves. Thus the church in Rome had begun to be an asylum for all society, and in a very literal sense the Pope fed the people.

The organization of this charity partook almost of the nature of an exact science. On the one hand, the Pope was the richest individual in Italy. The church had large possessions in Sicily, Campania, southern Italy, Corsica, Sardinia, Dalmatia, Illyricum, and Gaul. These estates were all managed from Rome, and the amount of correspondence which the Pope himself accomplished can be properly appreciated only by those who examine the letters which Gregory has left behind him. But the collection of the revenues was only a small portion of the task. The distribution was even more arduous. A sort of record seems to have been kept in Rome, an index of all persons and their needs; and so abject was the poverty of the times that the book seems to have contained the names of almost all the inhabitants of the city. On the first of each month there was a distribution of meal, clothing, and money. And every day there were sent out from the Papal Palace a large number of cooked rations. We must not think of the arrangements as those of a machine, with which Gregory had nothing to do. So personal was the conduct of affairs that in individual cases he chose especially delicate dishes for those who in their earlier days had been accustomed to finer things. It was Gregory who felt responsible for all these details; and when it was reported to him one day that a beggar had died of starvation in the streets of Rome, his remorse was terrible.

But in spite of these activities, and those even more serious ones of which we shall speak in a moment, he found time for the cultivation of music, and remodeled the liturgy, changing the music from the Greek tetrachord to the octave, and founding two schools of singers, one at the Lateran and one at Saint Peter's. And all this work was accomplished by a man who was physically unfit. The excessive fastings and privations of his life had induced in these latter years gout and dyspepsia; and much of his work was done lying on his bed. He even conducted choir practice in this position, and by the assistance of a long rod trained the choir-boys in the way they should go.

But if his life be judged as a whole, all these are seen to be only incidental things. His great work was that which was forced upon him by the political condition of Rome. The isolation of Rome, which had begun even before the founding of Constantinople, had now reached its climax. She was cut off from Constantinople, not only by geographical distance, but also by the indifference of the Emperor; and she was separated from Ravenna and the Exarch by the presence of the unspeakable Lombards. Nor was it any great extent of territory which Rome might call her own. The Lombards were certainly at Viterbo, and probably at Narni, and very close to Palestrina and Tivoli; and they were constantly pressing forward, so that Rome never knew from which quarter the attack might come.

Thus, in 592, Rome was threatened by Ariulf, the Duke of Spoleto, but in July, Gregory concluded a peace with him, and Rome was for the moment saved. When news of this separate peace reached the Emperor, he was angry, and bade Romanus, the Exarch at Ravenna, march to the defense of Rome. Romanus was very successful. He recovered from the Lombards several important towns, including Perugia, and then returned again to Ravenna. Thus Gregory's interference had prevailed where his petitions had failed.

Meantime Agilulf, the King, had succeeded in putting down the insurrection of the dukes, and he now crossed the river Po, and proceeded with a strong army against Perugia. After a short siege the town surrendered, and then began the Lombard march on Rome. The news of their coming was heralded to the anxious Romans by the arrival of straggling fugitives, who in several cases had had their arms cut off by the Lombards. Then Gregory prepared to defend the city, but for some unknown reason no serious siege was undertaken, and Agilulf led his forces back to Milan. One chronicler tells us that he did this, overcome by the prayers and entreaties of Gregory, who met him on the steps of Saint Peter's. But whatever the cause was, Agilulf retreated.

For five years longer Gregory's life lasted. It was the same sort of life that it had always been, the same activity as steward of the Patrimony of Saint Peter, peacemaker between Lombards, Exarch, and Emperor, and defender of the dignity of his beloved city of Rome. We have no time to enter into his conflicts with the Emperor Maurice, regarding the questions as to whether soldiers should become monks; or whether the Bishop of Constantinople should be allowed the title of Œcumenical or Universal Bishop. We do not need to linger over the sad spectacle of Gregory's congratulation to Phocas, who gained the throne, and thereupon murdered Maurice and his kindred. On March 11, 604, his life of action and suffering came to an end. Like Paul, and Augustine, before him, he was doubtless a great saint, but he was unquestionably a still greater Roman. He had not only saved Rome from the Lombards; he had saved her also from the domination of the Eastern Empire. Henceforth Rome and the Bishop of Rome were identical; and it was only a matter of time till Rome should be free. In point of fact, almost two hundred years elapsed before the coronation of Charlemagne, but an empire which was to last for a thousand years could not spring up overnight. At Gregory's death the principles, which were to make that empire, were already implicitly present.

Thus a body politic was formed in which the body politic of ancient Rome could live on; and thus was fulfilled the last requirement which paganism could well make of Christianity, the preservation, not only of her culture, her content, but also of her outward form. It is very easy to see the evil which the Holy Roman Empire accomplished; it is not so easy to realize the hopeless, helpless void, which its absence would have caused — but a discussion of these things would carry us beyond the bounds of our present task.

Thus our experiment is complete; and its main result is this. During the millennium and a half, from the foundation of Rome until the death of Gregory the Great, we have observed the presence of two factors: a permanent religious need, and a permanent religious supply. We have seen chronicled the rise of a series of instincts: physical, patriotic, superstitious, individualistic. We have seen their action and reaction; we have observed the various beliefs by which they satisfied their spiritual hunger. We have, in a word, recognized the normality of the religious instinct, even though that normal instinct be often, nay, perhaps more often, used abnormally. Above all, we have seen the great rôle which religion of necessity plays in human life.

We are confronted to-day by a very grave problem, the so-called problem of socialism; but possibly we are confronted by a still more grave problem, that of leading men to the satisfaction of that religious longing, which is quite as obvious a phenomenon of our present day as is social unrest. And in view of all that we have seen in these centuries of human experience, which we have passed in review, it would not be surprising if it should prove to be the case that these two problems are intimately connected, and that the normal relation of each man to his brother men — or such an approxima-tion to this normal relation as will ever be possible in this present world — can be obtained only by establish-ing the normal relation of men to those forces in human life which we subsume under the rubric of religion.

Nothing but good can ultimately succeed; and the good of socialism lies in what it can teach the individual. It may well prove to be an expensive and painful way of correcting and educating the individual; but if it is effi-cient, the world can afford it. But we may also find that there are ways of teaching these same lessons which may yet come into being, and may work side by side with the socialistic pedagogy, not eliminating it altogether, but teaching to many the same lessons in a more permanent and less painful and extravagant way.

For there are religious forces at work in the world, as there always have been; and these forces are, as always intimately adapted to the needs of the day, our own present day with its own peculiar problems.

INDEX

INDEX